First World War
and Army of Occupation
War Diary
France, Belgium and Germany

46 DIVISION
Divisional Troops
178 Machine Gun Company
8 February 1917 - 28 February 1918

WO95/2679/3

The Naval & Military Press Ltd
www.nmarchive.com
Published in association with The National Archives

Published by

The Naval & Military Press Ltd

Unit 10 Ridgewood Industrial Park,

Uckfield, East Sussex,

TN22 5QE England

Tel: +44 (0) 1825 749494

www.naval-military-press.com

www.nmarchive.com

This diary has been reprinted in facsimile from the original. Any imperfections are inevitably reproduced and the quality may fall short of modern type and cartographic standards.

© **Crown Copyright**
Images reproduced by permission of The National Archives, London, England, 2015.

Contents

Document type	Place/Title	Date From	Date To
Heading	WO95/2679/3 178 Machine Gun Company		
Heading	War Diary of 178 Machine Gun Company From Feb 8th 1917 To March 31 1917		
War Diary	Grantham	08/02/1917	08/02/1917
War Diary	Aldershot	08/02/1917	19/03/1917
War Diary	Havre	20/03/1917	26/03/1917
War Diary	Bourceq	28/03/1917	28/03/1917
Miscellaneous	O.C. 178 M.G. Coy	24/03/1917	24/03/1917
Miscellaneous	178 Machine Gun Coy. Company.	23/03/1917	23/03/1917
Heading	War Diary of 178 Machine Gun Company From 1st April 1917 To 30th April 1917. (Volume II)		
War Diary	Norrent Fontes	02/04/1917	13/04/1917
War Diary	Busnes	14/04/1917	17/04/1917
War Diary	La Beuvriere	18/04/1917	21/04/1917
War Diary	Sains-En-Gohelle	22/04/1917	30/04/1917
Heading	War Diary of 178 Machine Gun Company From 1st May 1917 To 31 May 1917 Volume. 3		
War Diary	Sains-En-Gohelle	01/05/1917	31/05/1917
Heading	178 Machine Gun Company War Diary 1 June 1917 To 30 June 1917		
War Diary	Sains-En-Gohelle	01/06/1917	30/06/1917
Miscellaneous	O.C. 178th M.G. Coy	06/06/1917	06/06/1917
Miscellaneous	Fire Orders for Barrage Groups.	03/06/1917	03/06/1917
Miscellaneous	Communications Appendix I	06/06/1917	06/06/1917
Miscellaneous	O.C. 178th M.G. Coy	06/06/1917	06/06/1917
Miscellaneous	Fire Orders for Barrage Guns.	27/06/1917	27/06/1917
Miscellaneous	Fir Mg Orders 178 M.G. Company.		
Miscellaneous	S.O.S. Line 178 M.G Company.	27/06/1917	27/06/1917
Miscellaneous	Firing Order.	29/06/1917	29/06/1917
Miscellaneous	O.C. 178th Coy	27/06/1917	27/06/1917
Miscellaneous	A Form. Messages And Signals.		
Miscellaneous	A Form. Messages And Signals.	28/06/1917	28/06/1917
Miscellaneous	O.C. 178 Coy M.G. Corps	29/06/1917	29/06/1917
Operation(al) Order(s)	Orders For Machine Gun Barrages In Connection With 46th Division Order No. 210	29/06/1917	29/06/1917
Operation(al) Order(s)	46th Division Order No. 210	29/06/1917	29/06/1917
Heading	War Diary Of 178th Machine Gun Company From 1st July 1917 To 31st July 1917 Vol 6		
War Diary	Sains-En-Gohelle	01/07/1917	04/07/1917
War Diary	Ourton	05/07/1917	24/07/1917
War Diary	Verquin Nazingarbe	25/07/1917	27/07/1917
War Diary	Mazingarbe	28/07/1917	31/07/1917
Heading	War Diary Of 178 Machine Gun Company. From 1st August 1917 To 31st August 1917 Vol 7		
War Diary	Mazingarbe	01/08/1917	31/08/1917
Heading	War Diary Of 178 M.G. Company From 1st Sept 1917 To 30th Sept. 1917		
War Diary	Mazingarbe	01/09/1917	30/09/1917
Heading	War Diary Of 178 Machine Gun Coy From Oct 1,1917 To Oct 31,1917		

War Diary	Mazingarbe	01/10/1917	31/10/1917
Heading	War Diary of 178 M.G. Coy From 1st-30th November 1917 Vol 10		
War Diary	Mazingarbe	01/11/1917	17/11/1917
War Diary	Noyelles	18/11/1917	30/11/1917
Heading	War Diary of 178 Machine Gun Coy. For 1st-31st December 1917 Vol 11		
War Diary	Noyelles	01/12/1917	31/12/1917
Heading	War Diary of 178 M.G. Coy From 1st-31st January 1918 Vol 12		
War Diary	Noyelles	01/01/1918	24/01/1918
War Diary	Chozues	25/01/1918	31/01/1918
Heading	War Diary of 178 M.G. Coy For 1st-28th February.		
War Diary	Cholues	01/02/1918	07/02/1918
War Diary	Hurionville	08/02/1918	08/02/1918
War Diary	Beaumetz Les Aires	09/02/1918	28/02/1918
Heading	War Diary of 178 M.G. Coy For 1st-28th February		
War Diary	Cholues	01/02/1918	07/02/1918
War Diary	Hurionville	08/02/1918	08/02/1918
War Diary	Beaumetz Les Aires	09/02/1918	28/02/1918

wo/95/2679/3

178 Machine Gun Company

War Diary

of

178 Machine Gun Company

from Feb 8th 1917 to March 31. 1917

Original

Army Form C. 2118.

WAR DIARY
or
INTELLIGENCE SUMMARY
(Erase heading not required.)

M8 Machine Gun Co.

No 1 / 4 2

Instructions regarding War Diaries and Intelligence Summaries are contained in F. S. Regs., Part II. and the Staff Manual respectively. Title Pages will be prepared in manuscript.

Place	Date	Hour	Summary of Events and Information	Remarks and references to Appendices
Grantham	1917 Feb 8		Entrained for Aldershot.	
Aldershot	Feb 8 – Feb 19		Arrived at Aldershot and marched to No I Camp, Thornhill Hutments, and attached to Headquarter Duties, Army Service Corps, for Discipline. The Coy were rather in difficulties owing to want of training of the Second in Command and the C.Q.M.S. in dealing direct with Ordnance and other departments. These were however soon overcome. The value of having bootmakers, haircutters, tailors etc in the Company was constantly arising & these specialists did good work and saved public money. Acting Col. died in Connaught Hospital on the 15th from rheumatic fever & pericarditis. Lt Hargraves Capt	
Aldershot	Feb 20.		After being fully prepared to go, the departure of the Coy Overseas was postponed owing to a case of Rubella. From this date much advanced work was done, tactical exercises being carried out almost daily, which improved the mens health, physique and interest. During the earlier exercises, all except Gun Numbers showed a rather lamentable appreciation of M.G. tactics. The Junior Officers seemed to benefit considerably from these schemes. The animals became thoroughly hardened and the men improved beyond recognition	Lt Hargraves Capt

Army Form C. 2118.

WAR DIARY
or
INTELLIGENCE SUMMARY
(Erase heading not required.)

178 Machine Gun Corps

Place	Date	Hour	Summary of Events and Information	Remarks and references to Appendices
Aldershot	March 19	4.45am	The Company paraded to proceed overseas, reaching boat siding at about 5.30 am – strength 10 Officers, 173 O.R. 54 animals, 28 prs of wheels. Entrainment started at 6.0 am. and mules and majors were ready by 6.16. The train left at 6.50 am reaching Southampton at 9.10 am. The transport, 6 officers & 99 O.R embarked on S.S. "Cawdor Castle" at 4.0 pm. 5 Officers & 96 O.R embarked on "S.S. Archangel" at 5.0 pm.	
Havre	March 20		Both ships were berthed by 9.0 am. The party from S.S. Archangel left the docks at 11.0 am & marched to No 2 Rest Camp, Sanvic. The party from S.S. Cawdor Castle, disembarked the animals by noon but had to wait until 6.30 pm. for the last limber, owing to the mails having been placed on top in the holds. It snowed heavily all the afternoon. The first party had everything ready at the Camp and food and accommodation were soon available.	
Havre	March 21/22		Stores & Clothing were completed at Ordnance Stores, Havre.	
"	23rd		One Pte admitted to Hospital suffering from scabies	Kinkozama Capt.

2449 Wt. W14957/M90 750,000 1/16 J.B.C. & A. Forms/C.2118/12

Army Form C. 2118.

WAR DIARY
or
INTELLIGENCE SUMMARY
(Erase heading not required.)

178 Machine Gun Coy

Place	Date	Hour	Summary of Events and Information	Remarks and references to Appendices
Harre	March 24	5.15 pm	Left Sanvic Camp & marched to the Gare des Marchandises. Entraining started at 7.0 pm & the train left at 9.30 pm. The animals gave a tremendous amount of trouble getting into the train, the mules refusing to back in the darkness.	Orders attached Much Capt
	March 25		Train reached Candas where 220 M.G. Coy were left with half the vehicles. The train was put into a Siding where it stood 11 hours leaving at 1 am the 26th.	
	March 26		Coy reached Lillers at noon joined First Army & appointed to 46th Division which had not arrived. Proceeded to Bourecq where Coy was billetted by O.C. 19th M.T. Coy A.S.C. Good billets for men & horses, animal mules outside. Coy had travelled well and discipline had been excellent the whole journey. All the men arrived in good condition & good spirits.	
Bourecq	March 28	12 noon	Coy left Bourecq and marched to Monent Fontes where it billeted, coming under the orders of the Division which was beginning to arrive.	

Hushazand Capt.

O.C. 178 M.G. Coy

Please note that you will require to leave Camp at 5-15 p.m. and a Guide will report to you at 5 p.m. and conduct your Coy to point 3 & Ration Party to Point 4

Sanvic, Havre.
24/3/17

W.T. Niell, Major,
Commanding, No. 2. Camp.

17288

Officer Commanding 148 Machine Gun Coy.

1. The Company

under your command will entrain as detailed in paragraph 4.

2. O's. C. units must be very careful that every man in their units is told the station and "Point of Entrainment" before marching off. Most of the numerous cases of men left behind have occured through neglect of this precaution.

3. The entrance to Points Nos. 1, 2 and 4 is at No. 70, Cours de la Republique, and to Point 3 at the Boulevard d'Harfleur.

4. Entrain at { Gare des Marchandises / ~~Gare Maritime~~ } Point No. 3

   Time 19.00 p.m. Date 24th March 1917.

   Ration party (Strength, 1 Officer, 10 men) to report to the Officer i/c Detail Issue Store :—

   { Gare des Marchandises / ~~Gare Maritime~~ } Point No. 4

   Time 18.30 p.m. Date 24th March 1917.

5. Attention is directed to the "Special Orders for Units passing through Havre Base," especially paragraph 6, and to "Notes for Entrainment."

   Any further information regarding entrainment can be obtained from the D.A.D.R.T., **rue Jules-Lecesne.**

   The Orderly Room Sergeants, if any, should report to this office, as under, ready in all respects for immediate entrainment on being posted to the D.A.G., 3rd Echelon, for duty.

   Time Date

   The times given are the hours of arrival at the specified place.

Issued at

Date 23rd March 1917.

, Captain.
D.A.Q.M.G., Havre Base.

Original.

CONFIDENTIAL.

War Diary
of
178 Machine Gun Company

from 1st April 1917   to 30th April 1917

(Volume II.)

WAR DIARY
or
INTELLIGENCE SUMMARY

Army Form C. 2118.

178 M.G. Coy

5 of 3

Place	Date	Hour	Summary of Events and Information	Remarks and references to Appendices
NOREENT FONTES	Ap. 2.	10.a.m.	Coy Inspection by Major General M. Thwaites C.B. Commanding 46th (N.M.) Division. This was held in column of route along a road and the effect was disappointing. The day was cold & bleak & the Coy failed to show to the best advantage. Many of the rules laid down by the M.G.T.C. did not meet with the Generals approval and the march past was not well done. The Orders for the Inspection & the Generals comments are attached. See Appendix Capt.	
"	3-8		Training was carried out as fully as the weather would permit. Snow storms took place nearly every day + the cold made outdoor work unpleasant on most days. Permanent trackmen were attached in accordance with its G.O.O's orders. This reducing nearly all gun teams by one man. One O.R admitted to hospital on the 3rd with Hernia. One N.C.O sent to Div Gas School on 6th inst. for a 6 days course. One Gas helmet was drawn in, in anticipation of the issue of Box Respirators. MAJOR ELLWOOD (13th M.G.Coy) was appointed Div. M.G. Officer to date from the 7th inst. See Appendix Capt.	
"	.9		A Div. Route march took place from AUCHY to ESTREE-BLANCHE. The Coy marched third unit in the Main Body. Passed the starting point at 9.42 a.m. This necessitated parade at 6 am + we reached the starting point about one min. the before schedule. Lieut. been Sir CLAUD JACOB K.C.B. inspected the Division + O.C units were introduced. The Coy reached fields seen after 1. p.m. Gun out was 1000 yds. names 4 some drivers having out without whips. Order re MAJOR ELLWOOD was cancelled. No Div. M.G. Officer is now to be appointed. See Appendix Capt.	

Army Form C. 2118.

WAR DIARY
or
INTELLIGENCE SUMMARY

(Erase heading not required.)

Instructions regarding War Diaries and Intelligence Summaries are contained in F. S. Regs., Part II. and the Staff Manual respectively. Title Pages will be prepared in manuscript.

Place	Date	Hour	Summary of Events and Information	Remarks and references to Appendices
Mount Joule	Apr. 10.		Box Respirator issued + arrangements made for putting Coy through Gas Chamber to test the fitting.	
		8 p.m.	We received our first reinforcements from the base completing establishment with the exception of one Range Taker.	Kurkagawa Capt.
"	" 11		Coy went through Gas Chamber in Box Respirator under Div. Gas M.C.O.	Kurkagawa Capt.
"	Apr 11.		Orders received for the Company to take over the antiaircraft defences at TRIEZENNES & on the road between ST. VENANT and ROBECQ from 92 M.G. Coy. Warning was received of the impending move of the division	Kurkagawa Capt.
"	" 12.		No 1 Section left for ST VENANT & half No 2 Section under 2/Lt BRYCE left for TRIEZENNES at 10.25 am Both relief here complete by 3.30 pm + reported to Division by 7 pm. Orders for remainder of Coy to move here received at 8.0 am giving just 2t hours notice	Kurkagawa Capt.
"	" 13		Coy paraded under Lt. HAMMOND & proceeded to BUSNES with Div. Hd. Qrs. Lt FAY went over independently to ratify billets. O.C. visited posts taken over yesterday & reached BUSNES at 4.0 p.m.	Kurkagawa Capt.
BUSNES	" 14		Following have been made consequent on orders received at midnight. - Half No III Section under 2/Lt HIGHNOOD + No 4 Section under 2/Lt CARMICHAEL left at 8.30 am to take over the anti-aircraft defences at HOUDAIN + LAPUGNOY respectively	Kurkagawa Capt.

Public Works Committee 3.0 pm

Wt. W14957/M90 750,000 1/16 J.B.C. & A./ Forms/C.2118/12.

Army Form C. 2118.

WAR DIARY
or
INTELLIGENCE SUMMARY
(Erase heading not required.)

Place	Date	Hour	Summary of Events and Information	Remarks and references to Appendices
BUSNES	Ap. 15		O.C. and transport Officer visited detachments at HOUDAIN and LAPUGNOY. Left Coy. H.Q. at 9. a.m. and reached home at 7. p.m. It rained incessantly until 6 p.m. Both Sections well situated running smoothly. *Kinhazanus Capt.*	
"	16	3.0 p.m	One Cpl admitted to Hospital & evacuated with depressed scull. Notification received of eleventh officer joining Coy:- Lieut R.H.V.B. SAUNDERS from M.G.C. Base. O.C. had conference with O.C. 53rd M.G. Coy with reference to relief of guns at TRIEZENNES.	
		6.15 p.m	on ROBECQ - ST VENANT ROAD. Orders received to move tomorrow to LABEUVRIÈRE. G.S. waggon obtained for the move from O.C. Divisional Train. *Kinhazanus Capt.*	
"	17.	10.15 a.m	Move to LABEUVRIÈRE arriving at 10 p.m. Nos 1 + 2 Sections rejoined at 4.30 p.m. handing over to 18th Division (53rd M.G. Coy) *Kinhazanus Capt*	
LABEUVRIÈRE	" 18		Lieut H.V.B. SAUNDERS reported to Coy. *Kinhazanus Capt*	
"	" 19		O.C. + Lt HAMMOND visited Nos 3 + 4 Sections. *Kinhazanus Capt*	
"	" 20	9.0 a.m	Move to SAINS-EN-GOHELLE arriving at 3 p.m. No 3 Section rejoined at 3.30 pm & No 4 Section at 6.30 p.m. LIEUT CASHIN to hospital with MEASLES, 2 LIEUT BRYCE taking over No 2 Section. *Kinhazanus Capt*	
"	" 21	8.30 a.m	LIEUT FAY (2 i/c) left to take temporary command of 139 M.G. Coy (whose O.C. to England - sick). LIEUT HAMMOND became temporary 2/c, leaving No 3 Section to LIEUT HAMMOND. Reconnoitring of 137 + 139 Coys' guns as far as possible by day. *Kinhazanus Capt.*	

Army Form C. 2118.

WAR DIARY
or
INTELLIGENCE SUMMARY
(Erase heading not required.)

Place	Date	Hour	Summary of Events and Information	Remarks and references to Appendices
SAINS-EN-GOHELLE	April 23		SAINS-EN-GOHELLE shelled intermittently – one private killed.	
"	April 24		O.C. visited the Divisional line with C.R.E and Corps M.G.O. selecting 13 out of 15 positions required. Rather a difficult task owing to the broken ground in front and the necessity for using positions near dugouts. Line runs from N.5.c.30 to M.33.a.25.70 – Ref Map 36c S.W.1. Lens – following the line of the German support trench. Headquarters shelled again but the fact that one could walk about everywhere without being worried was very noticeable.	Kinkagawa Capt. Kinkagawa Capt.
"	April 25		O.C. went round with C.R.E and O.C. 466 Field Coy R.E. taking 3 officers from this Coy, & settled an exact positions & fields of fire. Hostile artillery was more active than yesterday.	Kinkagawa Capt
"	April 26		Received orders to send one Section for instruction to 136 M.G. Coy. on 30th	Kinkagawa Capt
"	April 27		O.C. visited 138 Bde Hd. Qrs & O.C. 136 M.G. Coy to arrange relief. Shelling in MAROC while returning.	
		4 pm	No IV Section under 2t CARMICHAEL and 2t SAUNDERS left to join 136 M.G. Coy. Meeting guides at BULLY GRENAY. Section from 136 M.G. Coy. reported to Coy. Hd. Qrs 98 M.G. Coy. at 7.30 am 28th inst.	

Army Form C. 2118.

WAR DIARY
or
INTELLIGENCE SUMMARY
(Erase heading not required.)

Instructions regarding War Diaries and Intelligence Summaries are contained in F.S. Regs., Part II. and the Staff Manual respectively. Title Pages will be prepared in manuscript.

Place	Date	Hour	Summary of Events and Information	Remarks and references to Appendices
SAINSEN-GOHELLE	April 27		Orders received from Hd. Qrs. for another section to relieve a section of 137 M.G.Coy	H.H.Lazarus Capt
	28		OC visited OC 137 M.G Coy & arranged relief of sections. 2/Lt HOGGAN + 2.O.R. proceeded to CAMIERS for a course	H.H.Lazarus Capt
	29		OC visited No 4 section & had two sections employed in firing a barrage the night previously. The section was working satisfactorily. It was in Support & quite comfortable. Nos 3-9 positions on the Divisional line were well on the way to completion the others not having been started. The CHAPLAIN GENERAL took the Divine Service Parade	H.H.Lazarus Capt
	30		The mixture of personnel at 178 M.G Coy viz Hd Qrs- Transport & 2 sections of 178 M.G Coy, 1 Section of 137 M.G Coy & 1 section of 138 Coy makes readiness to undertake any prompt action difficult. The relieved sections fairly need a rest + overhaul.	H.H.Lazarus Capt

CONFIDENTIAL

War Diary of
148 Machine Gun Company

from 1st May 1917   to 31 May 1917.

Volume 3.

Original.

Army Form C. 2118.

WAR DIARY
or
INTELLIGENCE SUMMARY

(Erase heading not required.)

Instructions regarding War Diaries and Intelligence Summaries are contained in F. S. Regs., Part II. and the Staff Manual respectively. Title Pages will be prepared in manuscript.

Place	Date	Hour	Summary of Events and Information	Remarks and references to Appendices
SAINS-EN-GOHELLE	MAY. 1.		O.C. visited 138 M.G. Coy & saw stoy section and then worked down to BULLY-GRENAY their returning via the light railway from LIEVEN to BULLY-GRENAY.	Kinlaganus Capt.
	2.		O.C. visited 138 M.G. Coy to arrange about sending up another section to help take over the new sector of line from the old Divisional Northern boundary, in front of LOOS, to where old front line joins new line.	
		5 pm	Conference at Bn. Hd Qrs of all O.C. M.G. Coys with G.S.O.I. & Corps M.G.O. to arrange defensive barrage & prepare for an offensive barrage	
		7am	No 3 Section left to reinforce 138 M.G.Coy. Strength 1 Officer & 24 O.R. Kinlaganus Capt	
	3.		LT HAMMOND visited No 2 Section & the Anti Aircraft Section in LIEVEN & found all correct. All positions were chosen for defensive rather than offensive work, area fields of fire were found small and restricted. The A.A. Section was working independantly & the amount of instruction received very small	Kinlaganus Capt.
	4.		O.C. visited 138 M.G. Coy & inspected Nos 3 & 4 Sections. Most Gun positions were inappropriately sited in or round shelled localities. An opportunity to fire on a German rounding party on day 2/3 had been unfortunately lost owing to relief just taking place.	
			Lieut R. Seafield MC awarded by the President of the French Republic with the LEGION D'HONNEUR- CROIX DE CHEVALIER. for work done during his previous visit to France.	
		7pm	LT PEACOCK, 138 M.G. Coy relieving his Coy; another Section from 13+ Coy joining 178 M.G. Coy. Gun positions for defensive barrage sketched with O.C. 136 M.G. Coy	Kinlaganus Capt.

Army Form C. 2118.

WAR DIARY
or
INTELLIGENCE SUMMARY
(Erase heading not required.)

Instructions regarding War Diaries and Intelligence Summaries are contained in F.S. Regs., Part II. and the Staff Manual respectively. Title Pages will be prepared in manuscript.

Place	Date	Hour	Summary of Events and Information	Remarks and references to Appendices
SAINS-EN-GOHELLE	MAY 5		2/Lt Sanders rejoined from 138 Coy to take over No.1 Section preparatory to going up to 137 HQ Coy. OC visited 137 Coy & inspected No.II & 4th A.A. Section. All gun positions seem to everything correct. Tour more positions for offensive "barrage" selected. A.A. section has fired on a "Red Scout" machine in the early morning, getting off 230 rounds before the A.A. battery opened fire. The amount of wastrels seem to be increasing.	Kinkajaus
	6		No.1 Section relieved No.2 Section which rejoined Hd. Qrs. No.2 Section from 137 Coy which had received rejoined its Coy, another coming out to 137th 9 Coy. Both relief was worked by day & Section back by 11.0 pm	Kinkajaus Capt
	7	10 am	Section from 138 Coy rejoined 116 Coy which was relieved on night 6/7 & has been at BULLY-GRENAY. No.4 Section rejoined from 137 Coy on relief of Brigades. No.3 Section remained in the line & passed to 139 Coy. OC & TO visited left Sector going round line with OC 139 Coy & visiting No.3 Section. No casualties but positions heavily shelled. One O.R. died suddenly from natural causes. Arrangements made with 1st Pl. Hussars about Lothdep Divisional line in case of attack	Kinkajaus Capt
	8		OC visited 139 HQ Coy who had just got their new O.C.— Major Matson. Saw No III Section. Arrangements made regarding return of Lieut Fay from 139 HQ Coy	Kinkajaus Capt
	9		LIEUT FAY rejoined Coy & took over position of 2/C. LIEUT HAMMOND returned to No III Section. Proposed visit to new Divisional line with G.S.O.II (MAJOR JOHNSON). Not of postponed; OC next night along old Divisional line has been made too high & conspicuous, & several of the emplacements have been made & several misplaced	Kinkajaus Capt

Army Form C. 2118.

WAR DIARY
or
INTELLIGENCE SUMMARY
(Erase heading not required.)

Place	Date	Hour	Summary of Events and Information	Remarks and references to Appendices
SAINS EN GOHELLE	MAY 11		O.C. + T.O. rode over in accordance with instructions from Headquarters to BETHUNE to visit the R.E. Workshops, about anti aircraft sights + mountings. Search was also made to find 93 M.G. Coy in NOEUX-LES-MINES concerning the same matter but they had apparently gone. LIEUT HAMMOND with AdjT of 1st MONMOUTHS, selected advanced Coy. Hd Qrs in case of alarm - situated on open ground SOUTH of WATER TOWER by MAROC - Map reference, Map 36° S.W.I. M. 8. C. Central. LIEUT DANGERFIELD M.C. Legion of Honour, + party on A.A. Course rejoined Headquarters. No III Section relieved No III Section in PIERRE Sector, passing midy 139 M.G. Coy. K.M Lazarus Capt	
"	12		Total casualties for week - eight. Reinforcements nil. K.M Lazarus Capt	
"	13		Nos I, III, + IV Sections took 2 Boxes of S.A.A. to each position of Div. line. Numbers left Billets at 8. p.m. No III Sector reached billets by midnight. O.C. No I, + SgT of No IV Section but then No 4 + sections returned about 3 a.m. 14/5/17. O.C. started from 15 position + worked right down to No 6. He got lost badly between 6 + 6 (Same place as O.C. I Section) + redoubled his tracks eventually to had to return via LIEVIN to LV to ANGRY CORNER - Map Reference. 36° S.W.I. M 26 D 8.2. He whole line had been thoroughly reconnoitred + apparently learnt by day previously. K.M Lazarus Capt	
"	14		A lot of Armour piercing S.A.A. was carried out on range at BULLY GRENAY. Ranges 15 - 50 yds. Target + loophole plate. Maximum penetration 3/16". K.M Lazarus Capt	

Army Form C. 2118.

WAR DIARY
or
INTELLIGENCE SUMMARY
(Erase heading not required.)

Instructions regarding War Diaries and Intelligence Summaries are contained in F. S. Regs., Part II. and the Staff Manual respectively. Title Pages will be prepared in manuscript.

Place	Date	Hour	Summary of Events and Information	Remarks and references to Appendices
SAINGHIN-GOHELLE	May 15.		Further tests of Armour Piercing S.A.A were carried out at ranges from 100 - 200 yds. Target 3g" soft plate: maximum penetration less than at shorter ranges. O.C. n°1 k.d. 13g M.G. Coy re relief of Section on 19th inst. Enemy artillery noticeably quiet.	K.M.Lazarus Capt
	16.		Orders received for 2 Sections to man Divisional Line permanently + to withdraw Section from PIERRE Sector. Positions to be taken by up 4 a.m on 19th inst. Relief of N°2 Section postponed for 24 hours.	K.M.Lazarus Capt
	17		Southern portion of line reconnoitred. 10 R to Divisional Area School.	K.M.Lazarus Capt
	18		N°2 + Section rejoined Hd.Qrs. N°3 + 4 Sections took up positions in Div. Line. Lieut J.H. BRYCE met with an accident + put out his right knee. Lieut C.A.R. HOGGAN + 3 O.R. rejoined from Course at Camiers.	K.M.Lazarus
	19		Both Sections in Div. Line visited. Alternative + A.A. positions had been or were being prepared. Lieut C.J. HIGHWOOD returned from N°3 Section to take over N°2 Section, Lieut BRYCE being admitted to Hospital	K.M.Lazarus
	20.		Total Casualties: 1 Officer, 3 O.R. (all sick). Reinforcements 10.R.	
	20		One hostile aircraft driven down by guns of N°4 Section landing in the British lines north of LOOS.	K.M.Lazarus Capt.
	23.		Lt Hougefield M.C. + one O.R. proceeded to five weeks Course at Army School HARDELOT. N°2 Section relieved N°4 Section in PIERRE SECTOR releasing it for an attack on May 1st.	K.M.Lazarus Capt.

2449 Wt. W14957/M90 750,000 1/16 J.B.C. & A. Forms/C.2118/12.

WAR DIARY or INTELLIGENCE SUMMARY

Army Form C. 2118.

Place	Date MAY	Hour	Summary of Events and Information	Remarks and references to Appendices
SAINS EN GOHELLE	24	4 p.m.	Nos 4 Section attached to 138 M.G. Coy and under the orders of O.C. 138 Coy. assisted from support lines, attack by 6th North Staffords on NASH ALLEY – Ref. map 36c S.W.I LENS. M.1 Central. Fire was produced at 2300 yards, and opened at Zero. Attack succeeded. K. M. Lazarus Capt.	
	25		Through night 24/5 morning of 25th bursts of fire were maintained. At 1 p.m. enemy counter attacked. Rapid fire was maintained on the barrage lines but observation was obscured by heavy smoke shells. Total rounds expended from 4 p.m. 24th to 5 p.m. 25th was 50,000 rounds. No.1 Section relieved No.3 Section in LIEVIN SECTOR. K. M. Lazarus Capt.	
	26		Throughout the week ending May 26, hostile aeroplanes were engaged almost daily by Guns in Divisional Line. No 4 Section rejoined Headquarters. Aeroplane rumbles transport lines from during two O.R. one fatally. K.M.Lazarus Capt.	
	27		Total Casualties for week 2: Reinforcements 8. K.M.Lazarus Capt	
	28		Anti Aircraft gun mounted at Coy Hq Qrs. K.M.Lazarus Capt	
	29		Preliminary reconnaissance of ground in N.17 (36cS.W.I LENS) by O.C. Coy & Senior Section Officer. Twelve forwards positions selected. K.M. Lazarus Capt.	
	31		Divisional line and CROSSIER SWITCH were inspected by the Corps M & O (MAJOR BASDEN M.C.) accompanied by O.C. Nos 3 & 4 Sections relieved Nos 1 & 2 Sections respectively in the Divisional line. Enemy aeroplanes showed very little activity since the 26th inst.	

Kenneth M. Lazarus Capt.

148 Machine Gun Company.

War Diary

1 June 1917   to   30 June 1917.

Confidential

Original

Army Form C. 2118.

WAR DIARY
or
INTELLIGENCE SUMMARY

(Erase heading not required.)

17 8 M G Coy Vol 5

Instructions regarding War Diaries and Intelligence Summaries are contained in F.S. Regs., Part II. and the Staff Manual respectively. Title Pages will be prepared in manuscript.

Place	Date	Hour	Summary of Events and Information	Remarks and references to Appendices
SAINS-EN-GOHELLE	JUNE 1	2 A.M.	Further reconnaissance of ground in M.17.f + e. Eight guns placed between houses at M.17.b.2218 + M.17.b.6331. An O.P. was arranged in house at M.17.b 3200 + till filling in the two houses mentioned above. Telephonic communication was arranged for them in the centre of gun positions to O.P. and 6 Coy. Hd. Qrs. at M.17.f.80 in CRIMSON trench which had already connected to batt. Hd Qrs. at M.22.f.15.0. No. 4 Section was visited on the way home.	
		9 a.m.	Visit C.R. FAY left to proceed to CAMIERS in accordance with orders received for this officer to report "for duty" with a view to joining the instructional staff". 2Lt W.W. HAMMOND became temporary second in command. K.M. Lazarus Capt.	
	2	9 p.m.	Party left under 2Lt C.A.R. HOGGAN and took up 178,000 rounds of S.A.A. to the Black Horse. This obstacle was rendered possible by borrowing Lewis Gun Hand Carts. Transport proceeded as far as railway in CITÉ ST PIERRE at M.17.a.2389 Following officers reported to Company :— 2/Lt L. DRISCOLL (South Wales Borderers) & 2Lr A.M. WILSON (Royal Scots)— both from N.G.C. Base Camiers. K.M. Lazarus Capt.	
	3		O.C. visited 157 H.Q. Coy regarding loan of 1 Section for raid on NASH ALLEY. No. 4 Section visited on return. Total casualties for week nil, reinforcements nil. K.M. Lazarus Capt.	
	4		No. 4 Section moved from PIERRE Sector to LIEVIN Sector relieving No 3 Section which returned to Coy H.Q. No 2 Section proceeded to PIERRE Sector took over positions vacated by No 4 Section	

WAR DIARY
or
INTELLIGENCE SUMMARY

(Erase heading not required.)

Army Form C. 2118.

Place	Date	Hour	Summary of Events and Information	Remarks and references to Appendices
SAINS-EN-GOHELLE	JUNE 4	9.0 p.m.	Following were taken up to delicate positions by parties from 1 + 3 Sections:— 198 full belt boxes, 6 B.F. Machines, 27 full water tins, spares, foods etc + telephone laid to O.P. All Emplacements were dug + camouflaged. Party reached H.Q. at 4 a.m.	L.H. Lazarus Capt.
"	6		Nos 1+3 Sections left Hd. Qrs. to take up positions for raid on HILL 65. Nos 2 + 4 + Nos 9 on German defences behind. Both Sections in firing position by O.C. K.M. Lazarus Capt.	
"	7	5 p.m. 6 p.m.	Nos 1 and 3 Sections visited by day. No II Section spread over the whole of the Divisional Line. No II Section departs from Divisional line to join 137 M.G. Coy to help the barrage in raid on NASH ALLEY.	Kukazarus Capt.
	8	6.30 p.m.	"Zero" time for raids on HILL 65, and NASH ALLEY. Firing tape for Nos I and III Sections attached. No II Section fired from MUSIC TRENCH — range 1900 yards — elevation average 6°. Rounds expended by Nos I + III Section during barrage 43,800 ~ by No 2 Section 25,000. I + III Sections visited by night. The Belt filling Machines gave trouble, + in spite of testing, appear absolutely unreliable. Guns out of six stopped continually. Results were not directly observed.	Kukazarus Capt.
	9		No firing by Nos I + III Sections. No. II Section returned to their positions in PIERRE SECTOR of the Div. Line + No II closed in to the LIEVIN SECTOR	Kukazarus Capt.

Army Form C. 2118.

WAR DIARY
or
INTELLIGENCE SUMMARY

(Erase heading not required.)

Instructions regarding War Diaries and Intelligence Summaries are contained in F. S. Regs., Part II. and the Staff Manual respectively. Title Pages will be prepared in manuscript.

Place	Date	Hour	Summary of Events and Information	Remarks and references to Appendices
SAINS EN GOHELLE	June 10		All sections and O.C. 139 M.G. Coy. visited by day. Found Barrels had, and 4x1" running shot. The asbestos had given trouble, wearing out very soon. Spare Barrels were collected from III & IV sections and sent up. There were borrowed from S.A.B.O.S. These were Mark I, Mark II being unobtainable. Total casualties for week 3, total reinforcements 10.	Kenneth Maryand Capt.
	11		Direct observation of the fire from Nos I + III sections was obtained by O.C. 138 M.G. Coy. and Slabs were observed to be falling absolutely right. Nos I + III Sections had received orders to stay in another 48 hours, in notification of this being received at Coy. Hd. Qrs. No III remain in same position. No II have to fall back holding from M 17 c 51 to M 23 d 3869. Canadian raid in front of ELECTRIC POWER STATION - M 36 b (map 36c St. LENS) supported by Nos I + III sections. Barrels showed signs of wear, and guns did not fire as satisfactorily as on 8th inst. Enemy aircraft very active during the morning. O.C. visited O.C. 138 M.G.Coy & some difficulty was experienced in getting definite orders about actions attached to this Coy. After orders for relief, were issued + acted on, Lt. HAMMOND received counter orders + have after to turn had dismounted (this was due to the Orderly missing his way) No I section returned for another 48 hours to the positions in COWLEN TRENCH, No II section rejoined Headquarters. No I section could not reach fire nearly four until daybreak. K.H. Maryand Capt.	

2449 Wt. W14957/M90 750,000 1/16 J.B.C. & A. Forms/C.2118/12.

WAR DIARY or INTELLIGENCE SUMMARY

Army Form C. 2118.

Place	Date	Hour	Summary of Events and Information	Remarks and references to Appendices
SAINS-EN-GOHELLE	June 12		Orders received for relief of No 1 Section, which rejoined during night 12/13 with LT HAMMOND. Total S.A.A. expended 103,000 rounds. L.M. Lazarus Capt.	
"	13		Coy. now second line at Bn. Horse Show to 134 M.G. Coy. L.M. Lazarus Capt.	
"	14		Range at MARQUEFFLES FARM reconnoitred with G.S.O. 2 L.M. Lazarus Capt.	
"	16		Capt DRISCOLL transferred to 134 MG Coy and 5 O.R. to 199 MG Coy. C.Q.M.S. to Hospital sick. L.M. Lazarus Capt.	
"	17		O.C. visited 138 Bde in view of approaching operations, for which they get 2 Sections from this Coy. Travel to 138 MG Coy where all arrangements were made. Both Sections to go to the same positions in COWDEN TRENCH. (M.17b). Hostile artillery very active all day. Total casualties for week 2. Reinforcements nil.	
		8.30pm	No 1 and 3 Sections named and 60,000 rounds taken up to COWDEN TRENCH by No 2 and 4 Sections L.M. Lazarus Capt.	
	18	6.30pm	Nos 1 and 3 Sections moved from the Divisional Line to COWDEN TRENCH carrying their materials by hand. No 2 Section occupied Divisional Line holding Nos 3, 4, 10 & 19 positions. LT W.N. HAMMOND took charge of the two Sections in COWDEN TRENCH. L.M. Lazarus Capt.	
	19	10.30pm	Zero time for attack on Slopes N. of HILL 65. The objectives were barraged by M.G. but not by artillery. The attack was successful and three counter attacks were driven off. The ammo fired well and the B.F. Machines gave no trouble. S.A.A. expended 60,000 rounds. L.M. Lazarus Capt.	

WAR DIARY or INTELLIGENCE SUMMARY

Army Form C. 2118.

Place	Date JUNE	Hour	Summary of Events and Information	Remarks and references to Appendices
SAINS-EN-GOHELLE	20.		Lt P.J. CASHIN rejoined from Hospital at Lt A. NOALL from M.G. Base. Lt HAMMOND returned from CONDEN to prepare for future operations	M. Laraine Capt.
	21.		Lt CASHIN took over No 2 section from Lt Wilson Lt SAUNDERS as Subsection officer. Lt NOALL took over No 3 section with 2 Lt HIGHWOOD. 2Lt WILSON rejoins Coy Hd Qrs. as Subsection officer to Lt CARMICHAEL. Approx 180,000 rounds S.A.A. taken to CONDEN in view of approaching operations. Preliminary reconnaisance of ground in M.18.a for positions to forward line. M.19.a 9585 to N.25.b 2687	M. M. Larains Capt.
	22.		Orders for relief of Nos 1 and 3 Sections received at noon and cancelled at 5 p.m. owing to further preliminary operations against trenches in front of HILL 65	M. M. Larains Capt.
	23.		80,000 Rounds were taken up to CORDEN TRENCH for the Preliminary operations against AHEAD TRENCH. Orders for further operations were selected as follows. Six guns on line twelve M.18.a 0033 to 1037 and six on line M.18.a 0555 to 1262. Four of the twelve positions were already made, otherwise everything had to be got ready. We heard that supply was at M.17 b 22.18 (Ry. map LENS 36° SW.) most of the surroundings having had good cellars but no dugouts were available for use.	K. M. Larains Capt.
	24.	9.30 pm	Total reinforcements 2 Officers & 70 O.R. Casualties 1 Officer and 9 O.R. "zero" time for attack which was successful. Amount of S.A.A. expended 26000 rounds	K. M. Larains Capt.

Army Form C. 2118.

WAR DIARY
or
INTELLIGENCE SUMMARY

(Erase heading not required.)

Instructions regarding War Diaries and Intelligence Summaries are contained in F.S. Regs., Part II. and the Staff Manual respectively. Title Pages will be prepared in manuscript.

Place	Date June	Hour	Summary of Events and Information	Remarks and references to Appendices
SAILLY-EN-GOHELLE.	25	6.30 p.m	Working party left Hd. Qrs to make the new positions. It rained incessantly and beyond carrying up as much material as necessary, the two exposed positions were dug and a sap dug to know nearest forward line, to allow pits to be put in one of these. A hundred pdr. rate tank was also put in one of the known positions. K.M.Sayers Capt	
	26	11 a.m	Orders received that 2 days had been put forward from 28th to 27th. No.II section sent off as quickly as possible with all guns etc to dig remaining positions. Nos 1&3 provided a working party but guns could not be dismounted.	
		2.30 p.m	2 day postponed to 28th as previously arranged.	
		5.0 p.m	Orders received for Nos 1 & 3 sections to dismount guns. Nos 1,3,4, sections worked all night making positions, dumping sea filling rate tank etc. K.M.Sayers Capt	
	27		During the day Nos 1 & 3 Sections completed their moves to the new positions. OC left to join three sections in COBDEN TRENCH, No 2 section having been attached to 139 M.G. Coy for the operations with positions at the junction of COBDEN v COLLEGE TRENCHES at about M.12.b.90.15.	
		8.30 p.m	Enemy artillery fairly active all night - all the men in good cellars.	
	28		Guns all checked at daybreak. AA gun mounted, but no hostile aircraft came over during the day. Everything was ready by noon and men returned to cellars.	
		7.0 a.m	Zero time for attack on trenches E of Recroix Hill. Guns firing well and giving no trouble. Rounds fired...	

WAR DIARY
or
INTELLIGENCE SUMMARY

(Erase heading not required.)

Army Form C. 2118.

Place	Date June	Hour	Summary of Events and Information	Remarks and references to Appendices
SAINS EN GOHELLE	28th (cont)		A very heavy thunderstorm broke out at 7.30 p.m. lasting all night and making the trenches very bad for rapid movement. The artillery fire continued active until about 9 o'clock but did not come dangerously close to gun positions. After ceasing fire all guns were laid on S.O.S. lines but no signals were seen. Kenneth M. Lazarus Capt.	
	29th		Standing by for S.O.S. which was seen & supported at 7 p.m. Kenneth M. Lazarus Capt.	
	30th	2.20 a.m.	Orders received about further operations commencing with a preliminary attack at 2.35 am. This did not affect our guns as they were protecting a different part of the line.	
		3.30 a.m.	All guns had to be moved to bring fire onto new line. One section returned to old positions in COWJEN TRENCH, one section stayed in same position + one moved to CRIMSON TRENCH. These moves were completed by 4.15 am. the positions in CRIMSON TRENCH been some distance away and had to be kind of protection from heather. The belt filling machines had to be freed up on a fire step	
		11.30 a.m.	Weather in zero time & 4.4 am brought up by signallers. All messages were sent to H.dqrs. at SAINS-EN-GOHELLE which meant several long elapsing before the orders reached the line.	
		11.0 p.m.	All complete returned from the line and returned to Railhead. Total casualties for week 1 O.R. wounded. Reinforcements nil. Total empties returned during month, about 200,000 rounds. Kenneth M. Lazarus Capt.	

To:-
O.C
178th M.G.Coy

Herewith fire orders +
copies of Appendices I & II
Please acknowledge receipt

K Blood
O C 138th M G Coy

W423
6/6/17
12 noon

Fire Orders for barrage groups

(I) All Tripods must be mounted in such a way that zero is registered on the traversing dial when the guns are laid on the R.O.:-

(II) A filled sandbag will be firmly placed on each leg of the tripod:-

(III) An auxiliary aiming mark will be used, a natural one where possible this for maintaining elevation. The luminous sights & a luminous watch will serve at night.

(IV) Auxiliary aiming sticks will be used for the creeping barrage.

(V) Elevation will be checked after half the first belt & then as frequently as possible, this will always be done after a stoppage.

(VI) Barrels will be pulled through after each thousand rounds also they must be examined during any pause in the firing.

(VII) Care must be taken to ensure that all accessories such as luminous sights, sight lamps, condenser tubes & petrol tins are brought, also flash screens must be used in exposed positions, cotton wool should be provided for the teams.

(VIII) The empty end of the belt must be prevented from getting soiled & all filled belts must be carefully examined:-

(ix) The protective barrage guns will be kept loaded with an especially well examined belt, two men being constantly on the alert for the S.O.S (A succession of red lights which all ranks must know) If an S.O.S is seen, Officers in charge will open fire when they hear our Artillery barrage re-opening, rate:- One belt straight off, followed by medium fire, one belt per gun every four minutes. Officers will use their own judgment as to when to cease, conforming to the Artillery fire

(x) The OC 139 Coy is supplying an Officer & 2 OR's for observation daily on first floor of house @ 16.17.t 35,00. Their duties are to keep a constant look out for any signals, unusual disturbances & any possible enemy massing. He will repeat any signals observed & report by telephone to OC 137 & 142 groups in 16.17.b & any other information. All four group commanders in 16.17.t.M. OC 18H) will ensure that a constant look out is kept both on line of T also towards Hill 65

(xi) All guns will be laid by an Officer.

3-6-17   A.W. Ellwood. Major
         OC 138 M.G. Coy

APPENDIX I. - COMMUNICATIONS -

I. By Telephone through Batt. H.Q at M.22.b.20.20. to M.17.d.70.70 (H.Q's B3 group). This group will communicate by runner to B4 group M.18.a.05.35.

O.C. 2 Section 178th Coy is establishing communication between his group B.1 from house at M.17.d.70.70 through O.P. at M.17.b.35.00.

He will also keep 2 runners at Battalion H.Q's (M.22.b.20.20) in case wire is cut.

O.C. No 14. M.M.G. Batty will keep one runner at group B.1.

O.C. No 11. M.M.G. Batty will keep a runner at Company H.Q's. 138th Coy. M.28.d.78.32.

178. B.1 group. M.17.b. COWDEN TRENCH
    B.2.   "   M.17.b.   "   "
x   B.3   "   M.17.c.   CRIMSON TRENCH.
    B.4   "   M.18.a.   "   "
    B.5   "   M.17.a.   COWDEN TRENCH.

138th M.G Coy HQ will be at M.28.d.75.35 where all reports should be sent.

K. B. Hood
OC 138th M.G Coy.

MACHINE GUN COMPANY, 138th
No. 4
Date 6/6/17

SECRET. Copy No 4

To:- O.C. 178th M.G. Coy

Reference Map 36.C.S.W.I. 1/20000

Position of Guns	No. of Gun	R.O.	Range	V.I.	Direction	Fixed or Traverse	Quadrant Elevation	Time	Rate of Fire	Remarks
B1	1	N2c3435 Fosse	1850ˣ	+22ˣ	81° to 76° Rt Creep		4° 15'	Zero+3 to Zero+60	From Zero+3 to Zero+10 Rapid fire at the rate of little less than 200 per gun per minute. Zero+10 to Zero+60	Guns numbered from Right to left.
N17+30,18	2	14	1950ˣ	+22ˣ	85° to 76° Rt Creep		4° 40'			
	3	—	1850ˣ	+22ˣ	76° Rt Fixed		4° 15'	+5		Creep is to be maintained by a tapping traverse. Rate of Creep = 50ˣ every 2 minutes.
	4	—	1950ˣ	+22ˣ	76° Rt Fixed		4° 40'			
B2	5	—	2000ˣ	+22ˣ	90° to 81° Rt Creep		4° 54'	Zero+3 to Zero+60	Zero+10 to	Guns numbered from Right to left.
	6	—	2100ˣ	+16ˣ	92° to 81° Rt		5° 15'	+5	Zero+10	
N17+5226	7	—	2000ˣ	+22ˣ	81° Rt Fixed		4° 54'			
	8	—	2100ˣ	+16ˣ	81° Rt Fixed		5° 15'			

12 noon

MACHINE GUN COMPANY, 138th
No. 4
Date 6/6/17

Willwood. Major
O.C. 138th M.G. Coy
6-6-17

Reference Map 36.C. S.W.1.

G.657/138

Fire orders for barrage guns.
Time: zero, to zero plus 15'.
Rate: Intense.

---

1. 178th Company barrage (8 guns): New trenches from N.20.c.25.85 to N.20.c.55.65 and to N.20.c.80.70. Then from N.20.c.85.65 to N.20.c.85.40.

   (12 guns)
   137th Company barrage: Trenches about N.19.b.80.40 to N.19.b.99.10 and N.20.a.10.20 to N.20.a.20.00 and N.20.c.15.95 to N.20.c.15.75.

   139th Company barrage (Five guns): Embankment and trenches from N.19.b.50.90 to N.19.b.80.40.
   The above guns will, from zero plus 15' onwards lay on their S.O.S. lines, which will be at least 200 yards in front of final objective.

   (12 guns)
   Ninth Machine Gun Squadron barrage: Trenches on mound from N.20.c.90.70 to N.20.c.90.10. Also trenches from N.19.b.60.70 to N.19.b.85.20.

   (4 guns)
   14th Battery, M.M.G: Embankment from N.14.c.00.50 round to N.14.c.30.00

---

2. The 139th Company will sweep with 5 guns from zero to zero plus 7' ALARM trench (1 degree right of S.O.S. lines laid down in G.657/61).

   The 178th Company will enfilade with 4 guns, ADJACENT trench, and the trench from N.25.a.90.35 to N.25.a.80.70; time: zero to zero plus 5'.

   (8 guns)
   The 138th Company will lay on their S.O.S. line and fire from zero till zero plus 15'.

   All S.O.S. guns will stand by for emergencies after zero plus 15', and will fire rapid if S.O.S. is seen.

---

3. After zero plus 15'.

   The 9th M.G. Squadron and 14th M.M.G. Battery will carry on searching and harassing fire beyond a line 400 yards over final objective till artillery fire dies down, and again during the night following attack, paying special attention to the hour before dawn.
   They will fire rapid if S.O.S. is seen.

   Colour of S.O.S. : succession of reds.

A. A. Ellsworth, Major,
D.M.G.O., 46th Division.

27th June, 1917.

Issued to - 137th(2), 138th(2), 139th Brigades(2), 178th M.G.Coy.
14th M.G. Battery, 9th M.G. Sqd., C.M.G.O.
4th Canadian Division.

Firing Orders. 178 M.G. Company.

Gun No	Bearing TRUE	Bearing MAG	Range	V.I. +/- Fo	V.I. yds	Q.E. min	Q.E. deg/min	Target	FIRE OPEN	FIRE CEASE	RATE
1	170	132	2630	—	—	514	8° 34'	N.20.c. 6066	Zero	Z+15	Intense
2	170	132	2630	—	—	514	8° 34'	" 6066	"	"	"
3	170	132	2700	—	—	551	9° 11'	" 4570	"	"	"
4	170	132	2700	—	—	551	9° 11'	" 4570	"	"	"
5	124	136	2800	−5	−5	604	10° 4'	" 8545	"	"	"
6	122	134	2750	—	—	580	9° 40'	" 8560	"	"	"
7	147	159	2400	+2	+2	403	6° 43'	N.25.b. 76	"	Z+5	"
8	145	157	2200	+13	+15	345	5° 45'	N.19.c. 60	"	"	"
9	145	157	2475	—	—	434	7° 14'	N.25.b. 95	"	"	"
10	145	157	2400	+2	+2	403	6° 43'	" 8360	"	"	"
11	124	136	2600	—	—	496	8° 16'	N.20.c. 4570	"	+15	"
12	124	136	2525	—	—	457	7° 37'	" 7080	"	"	"

After ceasing fire, all guns lay on S.O.S. lines

S.O.S.   178 M.G Company

Gun No	Bearing True	Bearing Mag	Range	V.I. H.	V.I. Yds	Q.E Min	D.M.I.	TARGET	REMARKS
1	126	138	2075	9	10	303	5°3	N147.4582	All guns will work for S.O.S
2	126	138	2075	9	10	293	4°53	" 4582	S.O.S in direction of R.E.
3	126½	138½	2150	8	9	331	5°31	" 5360	Rate of fire – Rapid.
4	126½	138½	2150	8	9	331	5°31	" 5380	
5	127	139	2225	7	8	365	5°55	" 6570	N° above is gun numbers on
6	127	139	2225	7	8	395	5°41	" 6570	account of diagonal Target
7	129	141	2375	1	1	401	6°41	" 7660	
8	129	141	2375	1	1	391	6°31	" 7660	
9	129½	141½	2450	–	–	434	7°4	" 95	
10	129½	141½	2450	–	–	434	7°4	" 95	
11	130	142	2525	–	–	469	7°40	N300 04	
12	130	142	2525	–	–	459	7°39	" 04	

24/6/17

 M. Vayanos
Capt

Firing Orders.

Corrected S.O.S.

Gun No	Bearing True	Bearing Mag	Range	V.L Metres	V.L Yds	Min	Q.E ° knots	Target	Remarks
1	116	128	2350	+ 3	3	383	6° 23'	N20a 2626	
2	116	128	2350	+ 3	3	383	6° 23'	N20a 2626	As before.
3	116½	128½	2416	+ 3	3	416	6° 56'	N20a 9017	All guns well wait for S.O.S.
4	116½	128½	2416	+ 3	3	416	6° 56'	N20a 9017	S.O.S. is succession of REDS.
5	117	129	2500	+ 3	3	450	7° 30'	N20a 5504	Rate of fire - Rapid.
6	117	129	2500	+ 3	3	450	7° 30'	N20a 5504	
7	119	131	2625	0	0	510	8° 30'	N20a 6500	
8	119	131	2625	0	0	510	8° 30'	N20a 6500	
9	119½	131½	2700	- 2	2	549	9° 9'	N20c 89	
10	119½	131½	2700	- 2	2	549	9° 9'	N20c 89	
11	120	132	2775	- 3	3	593	9° 53'	N20c 98	
12	120	132	2775	- 3	3	593	9° 53'	N20c 98	

N.Boam
29/6/17

Kenneth M. Lazarus Capt

Secret, Urgent   27-6-17
To O.C. 178th Coy

Ref 46. Div. G.923, dated 27-6-17
7-10 P.M.
    Please arrange to fire through night on places before wire is being cut. This will be by your Coy. the wire in front of ADJUNCT & ADJACENT.
You will not fire further South than N.25.a.70.25 and N.25.a.80.30

No patrols are going out.

AW Ellwood Major

7-30.P.M

"A" Form.
MESSAGES AND SIGNALS.
Army Form C. 2121.
(In pads of 100.)

Urgent

TO: GRIT

Sender's Number.	Day of Month.	In reply to Number.	AAA
BM 227	27		

Patrols will go out to ABODE TRENCH from 1.30 am tomorrow morning aaa You will not fire from this hour until further orders aaa Acknowledge by bearer.

From Place: GLORY
Time: 12. MN

(Z) C of Huggett Capt

"A" Form.
MESSAGES AND SIGNALS.

Army Form C.2121
(in pads of 100.)
No. of Message _____

Prefix SM Code GLA Words 16 Charge
Office of Origin and Service Instructions.

Sent
At _____ m.
To
By

This message is on a/c of : _____ Service.
(Signature of "Franking Officer.")

Recd. at 8 - P.m.
Date 28/6/14
From GLORY
By Sig Wilton

TO — GRAHAM and GR17

Sender's Number: AA 32
Day of Month: 28
In reply to Number:
AAA

Do not fire until you receive further instructions

acknowledge

From
Place: Ellwood ~~Allwood~~ Glory
Time: 4-55 PM

The above may be forwarded as now corrected. (Z)
Censor. Signature of Addresser or person authorised to telegraph in his name.
* This line should be erased if not required.

A.A.47 To OC 178 Coy
              M.G. Corps
29-6-17

Ref 46. Div. order 210 of 29th June
Please note that you will
be required to move four
guns to B.1. group, & 4
to about the C of CRIMSON
where B.3 was. you will keep
4, in your present right
group.

        A.A. Ellwood. Major
            H.Q 46. Div.

Acknowledge by wire to me
here.

SECRET.

G.700/8.

Orders for Machine Gun Barrages in connection with 46th Division Order No. 210.

                                  (less 1 section)

1.   178th Machine Gun Company will move 4 guns into old positions in COWDEN TRENCH, (B.1 group), and will barrage LENS - HULLUCH Road from N.20.a.45.90 to N.14.c.45.75.

      Four guns will remain in CRIMSON TRENCH M.18.a.10.35 and will also barrage on above line.

      Four guns will be moved to positions B.3, about the 'C' of CRIMSON M.17.d.70.70, and will barrage LENS - HULLUCH Road from N.14.c.45.70 to N.14.a.35.45.

2.   No. 14 M.M.G. Battery (4 guns) will move to positions at about M.23.b.70.10, and will barrage from N.14.a.25.40 to N.14.c.55.80.

                                          8 guns

3.   138th Machine Gun Company, will move to position about M.29.d.90.50 and will barrage on a line from N.20.c.75.75 to N.20.c.60.35 to N.26.a.70.90

4.   139th Machine Gun Company will not move and will produce a double enfilade barrage from N.13.d.99.10 to N.20.a.25.50. (6 guns).

      139th Machine Gun Company will with 4 guns barrage (double enfilade), on a line from N.13.b.90.40 to N.14.a.30.10.

                           (1 section, 178th Co attached)

5.   The 137th Machine Gun Company will not move and will barrage with 7 guns on a line from N.20.a.25.55 to N.20.c.50.80, and with 4 guns from COCKLE or COLONY TRENCHES on a line from N.13.b.75.30 to N.14.c.10.97.

      These barrages will both be double enfilade.

6.   The O.C., 9th Machine Gun Squadron will prepare positions about M.30.a., and barrage on a line from N.20.a.45.98 to N.20.a.80.10 with 8 guns, not further than 2000^x behind final objective.

      He will arrange positions for 4 guns to fire on main roads in LENS.

7.   Details as to co-operation of machine guns of 4th Canadian Division will be issued later.

P.T.O

2.

8. Calculations will be sent to D.M.G.O., at Headquarters, 137th Infantry Brigade, at 9 pm on the 30th inst.
Machine Gun Companies will arrange to replenish S.A.A. stocks early tomorrow night if necessary.

P. Thorpe

Lieut-Colonel,
General Staff, 46th Division.

29th June, 1917.

Copies issued to :-

137th Inf: Bde:
137th M.G. Company.
138th Inf: Bde:
138th M.G. Coy:
139th Inf: Bde:
139th M.G. Coy:
178th M.G. Coy:
No. 9 M.G. Squad:
No. 14 M.M.G. Bty:
O.M.G.O.

Secret. Copy No. 8

46TH DIVISION ORDER No. 210.

****

Ref: Maps, LENS, 36.C, S.W.1, 1/10,000,
and Special Map LENS (2), 1/10,000.   29th June, 1917.

1. (a) The Division now holds the line along ADJACENT Trench from about N 25 central, thence AGUE Trench to N 19 c 7.8 thence ADROIT Trench to N 19 a 10.45.

   (b) 4th Canadian Division on our right occupy a line N 26 d 4.0 to N 26 d 0.0 to N 25 b 4.2.

   (c) The German Division opposite us is 11th Reserve Division, - an indifferent Division with low morale, who have already been badly punished this year on several occasions.

2. On the 1st July, 46th Division will attack on a three Brigade front to secure the line from SOUCHEZ River at N 25 b 8.6 to N 20 c 0.2, ACONITE Trench and ALOOF Trench, thence to N 13 a 95.65. This line will be joined up to our original front line by COLLEGE, CORNWALL and COMBAT Trenches.

3. The 2nd Sherwood Foresters and the 9th Norfolks, 71st Infantry Brigade, are under the 46th Division for this operation.

4. Bombardment by Heavy Artillery commenced to-day and will be continued throughout to-morrow. Detail of bombardments will be issued to all concerned.

5. The infantry attack will take place at dawn on the 1st July: Zero hour will be notified later.

6. Field Artillery and Machine Gun barrage maps are being prepared and will be issued to all concerned.

7. Frontages are allotted as follows :-

    138th Infantry Brigade from river SOUCHEZ to road running E.N.E from M 24 d 7.4 exclusive.

    137th Infantry Brigade from above road inclusive to LIEVIN - LENS Road inclusive.

    139th Infantry Brigade and 2nd Sherwoods attached, from LIEVIN - LENS Road exclusive to our present left.

8. 2nd Cavalry Brigade Battalion, 9th Norfolks and 1st Monmouths will be in Divisional Reserve, located as follows :-

    2nd Cavalry Brigade Battalion   -   CALONNE.
    9th Norfolks   ***   ***   ***   -   CITE ST PIERRE.
    1st Monmouths ***   ***   ***   -   LIEVIN.
    To be in position by 2 am, 1st July.

P.T.O.

9. A preparatory operation will take place at 2.34 am to-morrow, 30th June, with a view to capturing the line N 19 c 7.8 - N 19 a 50.52 - N 13 c 35.02. This operation will be carried out by 137th and 139th Infantry Brigades under support of artillery barrage.

C.R.E will arrange that working parties in ABSALOM and CROCODILE Trenches are clear of these trenches by 2 am.

10. Orders will be issued as to times contact aeroplanes will call for flares. Flares will be carried by advanced troops.

11. If wind is favourable, O.C, 'B' Special Company, R.E, will project gas into CITE ST EDOUARD and N 13 at 11.30 pm, 30th June.

12. Correct time will be sent to Brigade Headquarters at 9 pm, 30th June.

13. 137th and 138th Infantry Brigade Advanced Headquarters will be unchanged: 139th Infantry Brigade Advanced Headquarters will be at M 17 a 3.9. Divisional Headquarters will not move.

14. ACKNOWLEDGE.

G. Thorpe

Lieut-Colonel,
General Staff, 46th Division.....

Issued at 11 pm.

Copy No. 1 to C.R.A.
2   C.R.E.
3   O.C, Signals.
4   137th Inf: Bde.
5   138th : :
6   139th : :
7   1st Monmouths.
8   178th M.G.CO.
9   71st Inf: Bde.
10   9th Norfolks.
11   2nd Cav: Bde Pioneer Batt:
12   O.C, 'B' Special Co, R.E.
13   A.A & Q.M.G.
14   A.D.M.S.
15   A.P.M.
16   A.D.C for G.O.C.
17   6th Division.
18   4th Canadian Division.
19   I Corps H.A.
20   I Corps R.A.
21, 22 I Corps.
23   File.
24/25 War Diary.
26   2nd Sherwoods.
27   No 14 Mbls Battery
28   No 9 M.G. Squadron.

Vol 6

CONFIDENTIAL.

War Diary
of.
178th Machine Gun Company.

From. 1st July 1917.

To. 31st July 1917.

Army Form C. 2118.

WAR DIARY
or
INTELLIGENCE SUMMARY
(Erase heading not required.)

Place	Date July	Hour	Summary of Events and Information	Remarks and references to Appendices
SAINS-EN-GOHELLE	1.	2.47am	Zero hour for an attack along main German defensive line. Fire maintained from zero to zero + 20 minutes and then Guns waited for S.O.S. signal. Hostile artillery very active all day, shelling positions regularly every twenty minutes - shelling too and wounding eight. She attack was successful, but enemy concentrated artillery and drove us out of post of the line captured. Infantry observers reported good results seen from our patrolling fire. Kenneth M. Lazarus Capt.	
	2		Intermittent fire throughout the day. Kenneth M. Lazarus Capt	
	3		Visited by 14 Canadian M.O. Coy about shell No Section relieved, and rejoined Coy Headquarters. No position to be taken over. Kenneth M. Lazarus Capt	
	4	1. pm.	Advanced Transport left for OURTON - 4 miles SOUTH of BRUAY.	
		6.30pm	Headquarters and No 2 Section left by motor buses for OURTON. No 1 Section left the line and marched back to BULLY GRENAY. Enemy artillery active against LIEVIN but only put a few gas shells over CITÉ ST PIERRE. Position left empty + all G.A. dumped in shaft. Kenneth M. Lazarus Capt.	
OURTON.	5	2.30am	left BULLY GRENAY in motor buses, reaching OURTON at 3.52 am. Transport pulled straight through from line reached OURTON about 4.15 am. Section billets its within twenty minutes. Two sections rested horses out of ILLDB and moved. Kenneth M. Lazarus Capt	
	6	noon	Major A.F.E. ELLWOOD MC, DMGO, takes command of Coy, Capt Lazarus becoming 2/ic. Kenneth M. Lazarus Capt	

WAR DIARY or INTELLIGENCE SUMMARY

Army Form C. 2118.

Place	Date July	Hour	Summary of Events and Information	Remarks and references to Appendices
MARCH	7		Demonstration at MARQUEFFLES FARM under C.M.G.O. 5 Officers + 5 O.R. attended	Kukayama Capt.
"	9*		Coy marched to BRUAY to see HIS MAJESTY passing through, but did not see him as unfortunately notice of postponement did not reach the Coy.	Kukayama Capt.
"	10-23		Training of Coy. This included an inspection on 14th by G.O.C. 4th Division + a Rifle Meeting on 19-20.	K.N.Nayama Capt.
"	24	9.0am	Company marched out to VERQUIN	
			Officers + 174 O.R. VERQUIN reached by 1.15 pm	K.N.Nayama Capt.
VERQUIN	25	7.50pm	The 3rd detail left for MAZINGARBE, the transport going with material to LE NOIRS FERME, E. of PHILOSOPHE	
MAZINGARBE		9.0am	Coy left for MAZINGARBE, arriving by buses + taking over from 192 M.G Coy, 5th Division	K.N.Nayama Capt.
		6.5am	to 3rd left to take up positions in "VILLAGE LINE"	
		2.0pm	O.C. Vickers Section with Bde. Staff B? M.G. Coy.	
"	26	9.0am	Worked at guns in the Village	
			Positions appear well selected but require great amount of work. Trenches very wet + muddy in places above the knees.	
		6pm	Italia Water Canadian C.M.G.O. re operations	
		11.30pm	Major Elliot to HQ. Orders to take up positions at Otto + Capt Kuyama assumes temporary command	
"	27*	5pm	Orders received to support CANADIAN attack on LENS with all guns	Kukayama Capt.

Army Form C. 2118.

WAR DIARY
or
INTELLIGENCE SUMMARY

(Erase heading not required.)

Instructions regarding War Diaries and Intelligence Summaries are contained in F. S. Regs., Part II. and the Staff Manual respectively. Title Pages will be prepared in manuscript.

Place	Date	Hour	Summary of Events and Information	Remarks and references to Appendices
MAZINGARBE	28th		Positions reconnoitred and selected - 8 in GUN TRENCH and 6 in BORIS TRENCH (both N. of CHALK PIT ALLEY - G.29 & Ref Map 36a N.W.) K. M. Saparis Capt.	
		9.0 pm	100,000 rounds of S.A.A. taken up.	
"	29th		Very wet. Visit to O.P. postponed. K. M. Saparis Capt.	
"	30th		O.P. selected on crest of hill just behind gun positions. Positions built — material taken up. K. M. Saparis Capt.	
"	31	5.0 pm	Orders received postponing operations from 1st Aug. to 3rd Aug. Weather very wet.	
			Kenneth M. Saparis Capt.	

ORIGINAL.

Vol 7

CONFIDENTIAL.

WAR DIARY.
OF
178 MACHINE GUN COMPANY.

FROM 1st AUGUST. 1917. To 31st AUGUST. 1917.

Army Form C. 2118.

WAR DIARY
or
INTELLIGENCE SUMMARY

(Erase heading not required.)

Instructions regarding War Diaries and Intelligence Summaries are contained in F. S. Regs, Part II. and the Staff Manual respectively. Title Pages will be prepared in manuscript.

Place	Date	Hour	Summary of Events and Information	Remarks and references to Appendices
MAZINGARBE	August 1.		Weather still very bad. Trenches getting into a very bad state	KMkayanus Capt.
"	2.		Weather still bad. MAZINGARBE shelled about 12.30 p.m.	KMkayanus Capt.
"	3.		Weather still bad. Orders for indefinite postponement of operations received. Indn Section Relief begun by daylight.	KMkayanus Capt.
"	4.		Artillery lecture at AIRE. Two guns assisted 139 Bde in a raid on trenches just N. of QUARRIES, firing from 1.30 p.m. to 1.30 a.m. (8,000 rounds)	KMkayanus Capt.
"	5.		Positions selected in PONT ST, about 6 (Map 36c SW3) for day firing	KMkayanus Capt.
"	6.		Suspected Spy arrested in BORIS TRENCH by L/Cpl HART and handed over to the 1st CANADIAN DIVISION. (Later information shows him to be an absentee). Weather improving	KMkayanus Capt.
"	7.		North half of Divisional Area reconnoitred	KMkayanus Capt.
"	8.		Lieut Baugenfels selected new positions about Q30 & 80 as some of guns in GUN TRENCH are not useable in support of a raid to follow the other operations. Weather stormy with a tropical storm at 7.30 p.m.	KMkayanus Capt.
"	9.		Weather improving. Situation normal	KMkayanus Capt
"	10.		Weather fine. Enemy artillery and aeroplanes more active than usual.	KMkayanus Capt.

Army Form C. 2118.

WAR DIARY
or
INTELLIGENCE SUMMARY
(Erase heading not required.)

Instructions regarding War Diaries and Intelligence Summaries are contained in F. S. Regs., Part II. and the Staff Manual respectively. Title Pages will be prepared in manuscript.

Place	Date	Hour	Summary of Events and Information	Remarks and references to Appendices
MAZINGARBE	Aug 12		Inter Section reliefs: the left sector relieved by day, the right by night. Weather good.	A.M.Hayward Capt.
	13		Early in the morning, four postions were dug as shelter for MINERS TRENCH and two postions were dug at H.Q. posn for Cap.¹ firing. A test of peace gas was carried out at 10½ Coy and the results seemed very satisfactory. A small amount was issued for A.A. work.	
		11.30 p.m	A raid was not supported by four guns placing a box barrage around the area affected. the raid was carried out by a party of 137 I.B. followed by a second party at 2 a.m. 14th, on German system in H 13 d (Map B E-NW) These guns were fired in the open in a small cup in the ground. Tripods were mounted over pit by day. Retaliation was small. Rounds fired 9,000 weather fine.	A.M.Hayward Capt
	14	7 pm	Coy H.Q. moved up to TENTH AVENUE about G 29 a 2040. The O.P. was established at G 9 d 0882 and the Gun positions were as follows 8 in BORIS TRENCH G795 5050 - 5060. 4 in GUN TRENCH G 80 a 93. 4 in MINERS TRENCH G 30 d 0375. A violent storm at 8.0 p.m reduced all trenches to a bad state, although the positions were cleared and remained fire throughout the operations. All guns were in action by 11.0 pm. The enemy artillery and aeroplanes had shown more than usual activity during the past week and seemed to know of the impending attack.	A.M.Hayward Capt.

WAR DIARY or INTELLIGENCE SUMMARY

Army Form C. 2118.

Place	Date	Hour	Summary of Events and Information	Remarks and references to Appendices
MAZINGARBE	Aug 15	4.25 am	Canadian Corps on our Right attacked until 70 N of bene reaching as far N as the Bois HUGO. Our guns opened fire at 4.55 and XERO (4.30) and maintained fire until 5.35 am (XERO +1.5) on the following targets:- Trench junctions at H.26.a.95.52, H.26.a.15.74, H.25.c.65.05 and line from H.26.b.50.10 to H.26.b.15.05, each with four guns. The distance in rear of the west slope of the chalk ridge was too great for observation. Rounds fell 65,000 to MINERS TRENCH the heavy Hy Artie falling all around the positions but still aimed right among the casualty - wounded GUN TRENCH was also shelled and BORES, both camp look kind.	
		10 am	S.O.S. fire was maintained for 30 minutes on same targets at request of Canadian	
		10.00am	Germans to the strength of about two battalions were seen proceeding in column of route in a SW direction along the road on H.27.D. Information was given to Canadian Fd Arty and Artillery fire was opened at extreme range from GUN TRENCH Battery of the enemy were seen to walk into this barrage and suffer casualties.	
		10.50 am	Germans to the number of 50-70 were seen to run back from BOIS QUATORZE in a NE direction	
		11.35 am	Germans were seen advancing in open order from N of Wingles to BOIS DES DUNES, in waves about 16 paces apart at about 200 yards distance. They continued to come across the open until 1 pm advancing for about 1½ mile SW. By this time the survivors reached their front line main trench. All approached was a few centimetres across the top until they reached their front and second line. All guns were firing on these targets all the while especially shells they were inclined to burst too low through the slight ones Shrapnel guns fired direct, the others indirect fire been directed from the OP where the targets of day was clearly visible. Targets were placed on the large scale map and communicated by telephone to the indirect guns.	

Army Form C. 2118.

WAR DIARY
or
INTELLIGENCE SUMMARY

(Erase heading not required.)

Place	Date	Hour	Summary of Events and Information	Remarks and references to Appendices
MAZINGARBE	August 15 (cont?)	4.30 p.m	S.O.S. lines were changed by Canadian Bde to a frontal barrage with four guns from H 25 d 59 6, H 25 b 82 and an enfilade barrage with B guns from H 26 d 01 to H 26 c 9 65.	
			Guns fire on S.O.S lines in response to signals at 6.20 p.m; 8.56 p.m; 11.30 pm LMkayamo Capt.	
	16.	4 a.m	All guns fired in response to an S.O.S call.	
		4.30 pm	Guns open fire for S.O.S signal but no activity developed.	
		11.45 pm	All guns except the four in Gun Trench were temporarily switched off then last 52 minutes to K support a raid by the 5th Batt. Warwickshire Regt. Fire lasting 52 minutes was brought to bear on S.W. Corner of Hughtrap in H 14 c – trench from H 13 b 2020 to 2552, & road from H 13 t 6060 to 9560 – each with four guns. LMkayamo Capt.	
	17.	12.30 am	In accn as the raid was finished all guns heard of only replied to Canadians put up the Red Signals, do Canadian Inf call authority.	
		5.15 am	The guns from MINERS + GUN TRENCHES have dismounted and taken to Rear normal positions in the Divisional Line.	
			Four guns from BORIS bay dismounted & the section proceeded to next Gun Position four new guns on S.O.S. pales. Shi Gun mounted at V34 was laid on Canadian S.O.S lines.	
		4.30 pm	Coy Headquarters returned to MAZINGARBE. Total SAA expended 225,000 of which 30,000 was fired during the raid.	

Cont

WAR DIARY or INTELLIGENCE SUMMARY

Army Form C. 2118.

(Erase heading not required.)

Instructions regarding War Diaries and Intelligence Summaries are contained in F.S. Regs., Part II. and the Staff Manual respectively. Title Pages will be prepared in manuscript.

Place	Date	Hour	Summary of Events and Information	Remarks and references to Appendices
NAZINGARBE	17 (cont)		Total casualties from 14th inst Officers—nil O.R. 2 killed — one died of wounds — 2 wounded (1 accidental) All the killed and two wounded being from the Section on Gun TRENCH owing to a shell falling right on a dug out. The ammunition at all guns available during the operations. Belt filling machines could not be set up + all filling was by hand. K.Nakayama Capt	
	18	9.00pm	All guns in village have been permanent PGF fires to thicken artillery barrage. No four guns in South sector of village have begun a belt harassing fire on Enemy distribution to or N.E. side of front on G.5 a.A. in cooperation with 4 guns of 46th Division + guns of 2nd Division. Fire maintained at intervals from 9.00pm until 4.30am 19/R Rounds expended 13,000. K.Nakayama C/U	
	19		Situation much quieter. No food Heather Continued. Strength of Coy 11 Officers, 168 O.R. 1 Lewis Gun (attached) Continued — Rounds fired 13,350. K.Nakayama Capt	
	20		Situation in front returned. By day weather good, Night fine — boom boom, our right wing — boom boom K.Nakayama Capt	
	21		Canadian Corps continued their offensive on our right and all guns shoot by S.O.S. signal or favourable targets but nothing developed. Situation on our front quiet. K.Nakayama Capt	

WAR DIARY
or
INTELLIGENCE SUMMARY

(Erase heading not required.)

Army Form C. 2118.

Place	Date	Hour	Summary of Events and Information	Remarks and references to Appendices
MAZINGARBE	Aug 23	8 am	Canadian Arty supported, but nothing further developed. Tornado fired 3750. Weather good. Night firing on dump continued - about 14,500 rounds for night. MAZINGARBE bombed.	Lt/Col Kakayame Capt
"	24.	4 pm	Canadian Arty call supported. 2500 rounds	Lt/Col Kakayame Capt
"	25.	9:30 pm	During the night fire was brought to bear on N.W.Q. BUMP and it was hit on the BUMP with John sections. Lieut. H. Wilson admitted to hospital	Lt/Col Kakayame Capt
"	26th	6:15 am	MAZINGARBE bombed. 15 bombs fell around 6th Bn. M.G. Officers kept Battn the positions S. of POSEN ALLEY. Dump exit & factories dug in O.T.R at G 15 d 90-60 for a Shipping patrol in connection with "BOB" O.R in Stansfield Road at G 10 c 50.90. Strength of Company 11 Officers and 169 O.R	Lt/Col Kakayame Capt
"		7:15 pm	Heavy artillery fire broke out on the night & two openings but no action developed	
"	27th		Situation quiet. Observation poor. Aircraft activity very slight. P. Dangerfield Lt	
"	28th	8:3 pm	Situation quiet. Six Ph. G.S. supported raid on enemy trenches north of HULLUCH at 8.3 p.m. Rounds fired 14,600. A covering battery of 2 Ph. G.S. established in positions dug on the 26th inst. P. Dangerfield Lt	P. Dangerfield Lt

Army Form C. 2118.

WAR DIARY
or
INTELLIGENCE SUMMARY
(Erase heading not required.)

Instructions regarding War Diaries and Intelligence Summaries are contained in F. S. Regs., Part II. and the Staff Manual respectively. Title Pages will be prepared in manuscript.

Place	Date	Hour	Summary of Events and Information	Remarks and references to Appendices
MAZINGARBE.	29th	1 a.m.	Five M.G.s supported a raid on enemy trenches south of HULLUCH at 1.0 a.m. Rounds fired. 13250. N°1 Section in BORIS TRENCH were relieved by N°4 M.G. Coy. 6th Div. P. Dangerfield Lt.	
"	30th		Transport lines at SAILLY LABOURSE shelled. N°3 section relieved N°2 section in V.31 & V.35 positions. Day quiet. P. Dangerfield Lt.	
"	31th		N°4 section moved to the North and occupied V.29 positions with 3 guns and R.57 with one. Day quiet. Air activity alight. P. Dangerfield Lt.	

CONFIDENTIAL.

WAR DIARY OF

178 M.G Company.

from 1st Sept 1917 to 30th Sept. 1917.

ORIGINAL.

Army Form C. 2118.

WAR DIARY
or
INTELLIGENCE SUMMARY
(Erase heading not required.)

Vol 8

Place	Date	Hour	Summary of Events and Information	Remarks and references to Appendices
MAZINGARBE	SEPT. 1		Day quiet.	P. Dangerfield Lt.
"	2		Day quiet. R.56 position taken over from No 139 M.G. Coy. Enemy aeroplanes active. Company strength 9 officers O.R.	P. Dangerfield Lt.
"	3		New divisional S.O.S. lines for M.G.S. received. Enemy aeroplanes frequently over our lines but flying over no engaged by A.A. M.G.'s	P. Dangerfield Lt.
"	4		Day quiet. Observers in Coy. O.P. report that enemy movement is materially confined to between 5 and 9 a.m. within M.G. range.	P. Dangerfield Lt.
"	5		MAZINGARBE was shelled in night. SAILLY LABOURSE shelled in the afternoon. Enemy aeroplanes very active. A flight of ALBATROSS with no details two were persistently over our lines of late. No 1 Section relieved No 2 Section by Lewis gun firing battery team and Lt Dangerfield.	P. Dangerfield Lt.
"	6		Coy quiet. Vichy rainstorm about 6 p.m.	P. Dangerfield Lt.
"	7		Two guns positions selected at junction of LE RUTOIRE ALLEY S.O.B.3.	P. Dangerfield Lt.
"	8	7.55pm	M.G.S. supported raid on enemy trenches No of HULLUCH from positions as follows V.21. Magazine, V.35, Two guns, junction of LE RUTOIRE ALLEY & O.B.3. Two guns. Zero hour 7.55 p.m. Enemy retaliation with M. guns, slight.	P. Dangerfield Lt.
"	9		The sniping M.G.S. dispersed a party of 17 of the enemy about 7.50 a.m. No 4 section relieved No 3 section in the right sector. Company strength 9 officers O.R.	P. Dangerfield Lt.

Army. Form C. 2118.

WAR DIARY
or
INTELLIGENCE SUMMARY

(Erase heading not required.)

Instructions regarding War Diaries and Intelligence Summaries are contained in F. S. Regs., Part II. and the Staff Manual respectively. Title Pages will be prepared in manuscript.

Place	Date	Hour	Summary of Events and Information	Remarks and references to Appendices
MAZINGARBE.	SEPT 10		O.P. reports no movement during the day. Intermittent enemy shelling around second line. P. Dangerfield Lt.	
"	11	11.45pm	Between 2.30 & 3.0 a.m. about 100 rounds were fired into MAZINGARBE from Eleven M.G.S. fired 16000 rounds in support of a raid by 139 I.B. between 11.45 & 12 midnight. No enemy movement seen. P. Dangerfield Lt.	
"	12		Sniping M.G.S. fired a number of times on parties of the enemy all of whom were seen to disperse at once. P. Dangerfield Lt.	
"	13		No 3 section relieved No 1 section in the left sector. S.O.S. fire from V.35 & V.31 positions tested & found correct. P. Dangerfield Lt.	
"	14		Sniping battery relieved. S.O.S. fire at V.40 position tested & found correct. At 10.20 p.m. guns at V.35 & V.40 fired about 1680 rounds on their left S.O.S. lines in response to red very lights seen. As nothing further occurred fire was ceased. P. Dangerfield Lt.	
"	15		Day quiet. Slightly harassing fire from R.67 position. P. Dangerfield Lt.	
"	16		Tested S.O.S. fire of R.67 position and remaining guns of V.31 and found it correct. Strength of Company Officers. O.R. P. Dangerfield Lt.	

WAR DIARY
or
INTELLIGENCE SUMMARY

(Erase heading not required.)

Army Form C. 2118.

Place	Date	Hour	Summary of Events and Information	Remarks and references to Appendices
MAZINGARBE.	SEPT. 17		No 4 Section relieved by No 1 Section in Right Sector. Throughout the night guns at V.4.b, V.35 & V.31 carried out a shoot on GALT ALLEY (G.5.d.8.6.c), firing 36,000 rounds, at synchronised times. P. Dangerfield Lt.	
"	18		Sniping battery relieved. This has observed little movement in the last few days. P. Dangerfield Lt.	
"	19		Positions at R.57, V.39 & 40, relieved by No 99 M.G. Coy and teams returned to Coy H.P. Guns at V.31 withdrawn though teams still remain there for convenience. P. Dangerfield Lt.	
"	20		Position at R.56 relieved by No 198 M.G. Coy. Sniping battery given up & guns withdrawn but teams remain in the trenches. P. Dangerfield Lt.	
"	21		No 1 Section with 4 guns relieved 4 guns of No 71 M.G. Coy in DAY 17. RESERVE LINE (G.24.d.3.5). Two guns of No 9 Section relieved 2 guns of No 71 M.G. Coy in CHALK PIT QUARRY. P. Dangerfield Lt.	
"	22		No 4 Section, and half of No 2 Section, with 8 guns relieved 4 guns of No 71 M.G. Coy in TOSH ALLEY, the teams living in cellars in LOOS. P. Dangerfield Lt.	

WAR DIARY
or
INTELLIGENCE SUMMARY

Army Form C. 2118.

Place	Date SEPT	Hour	Summary of Events and Information	Remarks and references to Appendices
MAZINGARBE	23		Day quiet. The 4 gun & 8 gun batteries mentioned on the two preceding days fired S.O.S. lines covering HILL 70. P. Dangerfield. Company through officers. C.B. P. Dangerfield Lt.	
"	24		Day normal.	
"	25		Day normal. No 3 section relieved No 1 section in Batty position. P. Dangerfield Lt.	
"	26		Day normal. Harrassing fire each night on Tr. BIS DU QUATORZE. P. Dangerfield Lt.	
"	27		Battery positions selected in LOOS TRENCH astride ENGLISH ALLEY and in the old GERMAN second line between HURRAH ALLEY and HYTHE ALLEY. P. Dangerfield Lt.	
"	28		Day normal. OC returned from CAMIERS. Lt PEACOCK reported from 38 MG Coy at 2/Lt. L Dangerfield MC assuming senior section officer. Harassing fire continued. A. Nelogamo Capt.	
"	29		Quite quiet to night. 2nd Lieut Dangerfield MC proceeded to CAMIERS for 10 days Lewis Gun Cse. Day normal A. Nelogamo Capt.	
"	30		Battery in 78H ALLEY moved up during night to new position in LOOS TRENCH about G 26 & 60. B.O.O. dump at new battery position commenced. A. Nelogamo Capt.	

CONFIDENTIAL

War Diary of
178 Machine Gun Coy

from Oct 1, 1917   to Oct 31, 1917

Original.

178 M.G. Army Form C. 2118.

WAR DIARY
or
INTELLIGENCE SUMMARY

(Erase heading not required.)

Army Form C. 2118.

Place	Date	Hour	Summary of Events and Information	Remarks and references to Appendices
MAZINGARBE	Oct. 1		Orders received for one section complete to be ready to entrain on 6th inst. for service overseas. No 2 Section being at rest was selected through Aitken office was available & Graham & Ur Swath detailed to go. Enemy aircraft particularly active – especially against our artillery machines. Rather fine. Strength of Company 12 Offrs and 158 O.R. — Kukaramo Capt.	
	2		Orders issued for inspection of draft of 4th inst. & entrainment on 6th. Kraft received of further ammunition against LENS. Day quiet & overcast. Firing night 1/2 29700 rounds fired on corjunction with the artillery on points eluded. Swept Lewis gun system. Kukaramo Capt.	
	3		Day quiet, weather unsettled.	
	4	10.30 am	G.O.C. inspected the section leaving the Company, he was pleased with the appearance of the men. He lit pleased with the appearance of the men. He fol. Pleased with the SOS barrage.	
		10 pm	Enemy shelled heavy bombardment all round Hill 70. Battery in LOOS TRENCH (G.36.c.60) 3000 to 4 opened immediately on S.O.S. lines (H.B.2 & 3rd) with n firing 15,600 rounds. This was maintained on enemy infantry reported that the attack of the British ? heavily shelved on enemy trench. They failed to reach our line. Kukaramo Capt.	
	5	9.30 am	G.O.C. writes from Sickens Transport Uhr. In LA GORGUE No. New followed. Bazan?	
	6	9 am 2.30 pm	G.O.C. Section again & addressed them offered to do The section entrained at 6.30pm inst. for MARSEILLES to two days rations. Kukaramo Capt.	

2449 Wt. W14957/M90 750,000 1/16 J.B.C. & A. Forms/C.2118/12.

WAR DIARY
or
INTELLIGENCE SUMMARY
(Erase heading not required.)

Army Form C. 2118.

Place	Date	Hour	Summary of Events and Information	Remarks and references to Appendices
MAZINGARBE	Oct 6		Weather very wet. Situation unusually quiet. Operations against LENS postponed	Lt.Col.Lazarus Cpt.
	14th	14th	Weather unsettled. Situation quiet & normal. Trench routine carried out.	Lt.Col.Lazarus Cpt.
	15th		Weather very unsettled. PHILOSOPHE & LOOS batteries heavily shelled in morning. During the brighter intervals enemy Aircraft very active, four hundred rounds being fired at low flying aircraft by our A/A gun	Lt.Peacock/r
	16th		Weather fine. Situation very quiet.	Lt.Peacock/r
	17th		Fine day. Enemy artillery very active on LOOS & vicinity. E. Aircraft unusually active. Eight low-flying planes crossed our lines in the morning, some of them opening machine gun fire on the CHALK PIT & on our A/A gun	Lt.Peacock/r
	18th		Fine clear section relief takes place. CHALK PIT heavily trench-mortared at night. Enemy Divisional Relief suspected opposite our front so heavy harassing fire was kept up all night on roads, tracks, dumps etc, 12,250 rounds being fired	Lt.Peacock/r
	19th		Weather wet & misty. Situation very quiet. Enemy artillery activity considerably below normal. Harassing fire kept up 5000 rounds fired	L/Cpl Peacock/r
	20th		Dull day, fine very quiet except for heavy shelling of HILL 70 at 1pm & 4.30pm	Lt.Peacock/r

Army Form C. 2118.

WAR DIARY
or
INTELLIGENCE SUMMARY

(Erase heading not required.)

Instructions regarding War Diaries and Intelligence Summaries are contained in F. S. Regs., Part II. and the Staff Manual respectively. Title Pages will be prepared in manuscript.

Place	Date (Oct)	Hour	Summary of Events and Information	Remarks and references to Appendices
MAZINGARBE	21st		Wet day. Fine quiet. New SOS lines received	R A Peacock L/t
	22nd		Fine. Enemy aeroplane brought down near PHILOSOPHE CHALK PIT again heavily shelled. Otherwise situation quiet.	R A Peacock L/t
	23rd		Fine. Exceptionally quiet day. Visited all the guns with the Acting DMGO. Harassing fire kept up.	R A Peacock L/t
	24th		Strong gale blowing. New section relief takes place 4/LT HIGHWOOD goes on leave. CHALK PIT again shelled with 5.9's.	R A Peacock L/t
	25th		Fine fine very quiet. Enemy artillery active on LOOS in morning.	R A Peacock L/t
	26th		Very wet day. Some of the communication trenches to HILL 70 over knee deep in water. Situation quiet.	R A Peacock L/t
	27th		C.O. returned from leave. Day fine. Situation normal. Marked aerial activity.	Kinkazarno Capt.
	28th		Night flying very much used by our airmen during the moonlight nights. Enemy artillery very active all around LOOS + HILL 70, as though they had seen a hostile relief or they suspected a British relief.	Kinkazarno Capt.
	29th		Two U.S.? officers joined the Coy for three days attachment are proceeded to CHALK PIT and one to LOOS. Enemy artillery + M.G. active throughout the night. Day fine and normal.	Kinkazarno Capt.

WAR DIARY
or
INTELLIGENCE SUMMARY

Army Form C. 2118.

Place	Date	Hour	Summary of Events and Information	Remarks and references to Appendices
MEAULTE(?)	30		The two R.S.A. officers explored the line during the day & reached Coy HQ about 7 pm. Interpreter robot worked. Day not misty. Barrage normal. Wirelogram Coy.	
	31	4:30h	Having spent the officers studied interior barrage Day hre Raid on hostile groups CHALK PIT, proceeded to a dummy raid at 4.28 pm whole HURRACH 9ho hostile artillery pres acts against. Enemy raid from YERO onwards She raid was successful and 39 Prisoners Captured. The Lots BATTERY was firing to the line half of ""Fid of" Fils"4" and Supports of the raid & fires 27,050. The CHALK PIT ALLEY gun fires on a trench junction just SOUTH of the was raided. Our R.R.A. officers saw the raid from the O.P. which he had & the Company during operation of August 15 and afterwards saw the prisoners at 154 Brigade Headquarters. One two & 9 prisoners of 1st line were from 15 years old.	

K.W. Rogers Capt(?)

Army Form C. 2118.

WAR DIARY
or
INTELLIGENCE SUMMARY

(Erase heading not required.)

Vol 10

WAR DIARY.

of

118 M.G. Coy.

From

to

30th November 1917.

WAR DIARY or INTELLIGENCE SUMMARY

Army Form C. 2118.

Place	Date Nov	Hour	Summary of Events and Information	Remarks and references to Appendices
SINGAPORE	1st		Weather fine. The day was very quiet. Strength of Company 9 officers (including 2/Lt Q.S.) and 146 O.R. (including 3 officers attached) Khazanus Capt.	
"	2nd		Our artillery was active all day, the enemy retaliating on HILL 70. Gas was projected at night & enemy gas alarms were heard, and an explosion was seen in HULLUCH. 2000 rounds were fired on gaps in the enemy wire in front of Hill 70. Khazanus Capt.	
"	3rd		Day fine but misty. Situation very quiet. Khazanus Capt.	
"	4th	5.40 pm	Day was fine and normal. Aerial activity small. Our fire produced by C/B(H.32 & 60) and CHALK PIT ALLEY GUN in support of raid by 139 Inf. Bde. Rounds fired 14,500. Hostile artillery + MG were active against the CHALK PIT & the area around the Battery. Khazanus Capt.	
"	5		Locs was shelled at 2 am and again at 3 pm. The day was fine but misty and passed very quietly. Aerial activity nil. During the night 5/6 the enemy MG and Rifle fire was unusually active though it all night, the enemy showing signs of nervousness.	
		10.15 pm	The POST N ALLEY Gun stood by to open fire in support of a "silent" raid by the Batt. 1.13 Shop. The raid was not called for. Khazanus Capt. Gutteridge relief took place.	
	6		The enemy MG and rifles fire unusually active during the night 5/6, and the enemy generally showed signs of nervousness. Enemy artillery registered on the CHALK PIT from 7.45 am until 10 am.	

WAR DIARY
INTELLIGENCE SUMMARY

Army Form C. 2118.

Instructions regarding War Diaries and Intelligence Summaries are contained in F.S. Regs., Part II. and the Staff Manual respectively. Title Pages will be prepared in manuscript.

(Erase heading not required.)

Place	Date Nov.	Hour	Summary of Events and Information	Remarks and references to Appendices
MAZINGARBE	6 (cont)		CHALK PIT ALLEY, then HUGO KATHE, the announcing trenches enemy aircraft were normal, there being seen to cross our line at HILL 70.	Kinlayames Capt.
	7		During night 6/7, 16000 rounds were fired in view of a suspected hostile relief. 9/7 night was otherwise quiet. Both artilleries + air services were active throughout the day. Information was obtained from a prisoner that the enemy might attempt to recapture HILL 70. No extra steps are taken to improve defences.	Kinlayames Capt.
	8		Day time. Situation normal.	Kinlayames Capt.
	9		Enemy heavily bombarded round PUITS 14 BIS during the morning about 1.30 pm WINGLES WATER TOWER & the FACTORY CHIMNEY were knocked down by our heavy artillery. At 5.10 pm the enemy put down a heavy barrage lasting 5 minutes on to HILL 70 our artillery replied vigorously.	Kinlayames Capt.
	10	9 am	Gas was projected by us during the night 9/10. the Division on our RIGHT made a raid + in retaliation the enemy shelled HILL 70. the day otherwise passed quietly.	Kinlayames Capt.
	11		The night was quiet except for our organized shoots. The morning was normal. At 3.45 enemy opened a heavy bombardment of HILL 70 with T.M. of all sizes, 5.9 H.E. + 5.9 Shrapnel this lasted until 4.30 pm. Aerial activity normal.	Kinlayames Capt.

WAR DIARY
or
INTELLIGENCE SUMMARY

(Erase heading not required.)

Army Form C. 2118.

Place	Date Nov	Hour	Summary of Events and Information	Remarks and references to Appendices
MATANGARAE	12		Situation relief took place. The weather has been tough, cold & misty. Harassing fire on & being kept up at the rate of 5,000 rounds every other night. The day was normal, with marked aerial activity.	Khukayaw's Capt.
"	13		Day fine. Situation quiet until 4.15 p.m. when the enemy opened a heavy bombardment of the CHALK PIT with S.q. light 12/13th. This lasted until 5.45 p.m. 3000 rounds were fired during the night. Strength of Company 140 O.R. + 8 officers	Khukayaw Capt.
"	14		Fine but foggy. Day very quiet.	Khukayaw Capt.
"	15		Lt CASHIN left to assume duties of 2i/c to 177 M.G. Company. Gas shells were fired into LOOS at intervals during the night. The day was normal with normal aeroplane activity. Orders received for Capt LAZARUS to report to G.O.C. M.G.T.C. GRANTHAM, & for Capt. ___ now to join the Company.	Khukayaw Capt.
"	16		Normal.	Newport/Col/Lt.
"	17		Hostile artillery active. Capt. LOW reported from 138 M.G. Coy.	Newport/Col/Lt.

Army Form C. 2118.

WAR DIARY
or
INTELLIGENCE SUMMARY
(Erase heading not required.)

Instructions regarding War Diaries and Intelligence Summaries are contained in F. S. Regs., Part II. and the Staff Manual respectively. Title Pages will be prepared in manuscript.

Place	Date	Hour	Summary of Events and Information	Remarks and references to Appendices
NOYELLES	18		Headquarters moved from MAZINGARBE to NOYELLES MAP "BETHUNE" 1/10000 L19 & 25.75.	
			Capt. LOW assumes command of the Company. Situation normal.	
	19 & 20		Weather fine — Situation normal	
	21		Raid by 11th Division on our right. M.G. of this division cooperated in accordance with scheme issued by S.M.G.O. Rev of this Company. Guns were employed — rounds fired 2200. The weather broke & there was rain all day.	
"	22	6.54AM	S.O.S. signal observed by P. batty at 6.54AM. The batty at once opened on S.O.S. line as follows:— Right Half Batty (4guns) on L14.4.70 RIGHT line, Left Half Batty (4 guns) on H11.4.40 LEFT line. Rounds fired 5500. Enemy artillery was active in the early morning. A review of attempt by the enemy. Throughout the day situation was again normal.	

WAR DIARY
INTELLIGENCE SUMMARY

Army Form C. 2118.

Place	Date	Hour	Summary of Events and Information	Remarks and references to Appendices
NOYELLES	23		Inter Company Relief carried out. Harassing fire carried out from now onwards under arrangements made by S.M.G.O.	Murphy Lt Col
"	24		Situation normal. 2Lt. HOGGAN reported from leave.	Murphy Lt Col
"	25		Normal. 2Lt SAUNDERS reported for duty from 1st ARMY ANTI-AIRCRAFT SCHOOL.	Murphy Lt Col
"	26		Normal. Lt CARMICHAEL reported from VETERINARY COURSE, A.H.T.D., ABBEVILLE.	Murphy Lt Col
"	27		"P" Batty 8 guns relieved by 32 M.G. Coy. An additional defence gun placed in LOOS TRENCH covering post in H.19.a. Maj. BENIFONTAINE ½ 30,000, 1 O.R. wounded.	Murphy Lt Col

Army Form C. 2118.

WAR DIARY
INTELLIGENCE SUMMARY
(Erase heading not required.)

Instructions regarding War Diaries and Intelligence Summaries are contained in F. S. Regs., Part II. and the Staff Manual respectively. Title Pages will be prepared in manuscript.

Place	Date	Hour	Summary of Events and Information	Remarks and references to Appendices
NOYELLES	28 -30		Situation normal. The weather during the whole month was few very good for November. Murphy Ralph	

Murphy Ralph
O.C. 178th Coy

Army Form C. 2118.

WAR DIARY
or
INTELLIGENCE SUMMARY

(Erase heading not required.)

WAR DIARY
of
148 Machine Gun Coy.
for
1st — 31st DECEMBER 1917

Vol 11

WAR DIARY
INTELLIGENCE SUMMARY

Army Form C. 2118.

178 M.G. Coy.

Place	Date	Hour	Summary of Events and Information	Remarks and references to Appendices
NOYELLES	Sept 1		"B" Battery, CAMBRIN SECTOR reconnoitred preparatory to relieving 74th M.G.Coy. "B" Batty. situated map. LA BASSEE 1/10000 A.20.B.5.2.	Musfardotoff
"	2nd		74th M.G.Coy. relieved in "B" Batty. with 4 M.guns. 1 O.R. Killed by aircraft bombs dropped on NOYELLES. Enemy also shelled NOYELLES. Our A.A.M. guns engaged several hostile aeroplanes. Musfardotoff	Musfardotoff
"	3rd & 4th		On both days over A.A.guns were in action against hostile aircraft. Situation normal.	Musfardotoff
"	5.		1000 rounds fired by POSEN ALLEY GUN keeping gap in enemy 3rd line were open. A.A.guns only fired 50 rounds.	Musfardotoff
"	6		Programme for harassing fire from "B" Batty. issued by D.M.G.O. "B" Batty. fired 2500 rounds during the night. On the Right Sector 1500 rounds were fired on gaps in enemy wire. A.A. guns were frequently in action against hostile aircraft. Forced landing Light, picked up near 200 S TRENCH.	Musfardotoff
"	7.		Interaction relief carried out in RIGHT SECTOR. 1400 rounds fired from RIGHT SECTOR on gaps in enemy wire. 2000 rounds harassing fire from "B" BATTY.	Musfardotoff

Army Form C. 2118.

WAR DIARY
INTELLIGENCE SUMMARY
(Erase heading not required.)

Instructions regarding War Diaries and Intelligence Summaries are contained in F. S. Regs., Part II. and the Staff Manual respectively. Title Pages will be prepared in manuscript.

Place	Date	Hour	Summary of Events and Information	Remarks and references to Appendices
NOYELLES	8		"O" Batty opened on its S.O.S. line between 5 P.M. & 6 P.M. on observing considerable activity on its line of fire. This resulted in an enemy raid being beaten off. Usual harassing fire carried out also fire on gaps in wire. 500 rounds fired by RIGHT SECTOR guns in support of a small raid by 5th S. STAFFS.	
	9-10		Usual harassing fire carried out & fire on gaps in wire. Situation normal.	
	11.		4 guns were engaged in a daylight raid. Temporary positions were chosen for the guns 2 in CHALK PIT ALLEY about 9.30 D.S.8 and 2 in BROADWAY about G.24.D.8.5. No casualties. Enemy's Barrage appeared to fall on our RESERVE LINE chiefly between POSEN ALLEY & BROADWAY. Usual harassing fire carried out at night.	MAP 100 S FOCUS 9A.
	12th		Usual harassing fire carried out. A.A. guns fired 350 rounds during the day. Shell gas attack on LEFT SECTOR and on request HARLEY STREET BATTY fired 3000 rounds on S.O.S. lines. 500 rounds also fired by RIGHT SECTOR guns on S.O.S. LINES.	

Army Form C. 2118.

WAR DIARY
INTELLIGENCE SUMMARY
(Erase heading not required.)

Instructions regarding War Diaries and Intelligence Summaries are contained in F. S. Regs., Part II. and the Staff Manual respectively. Title Pages will be prepared in manuscript.

Place	Date	Hour	Summary of Events and Information	Remarks and references to Appendices
NOYELLES	13	3.25AM	1000 rounds fired by RIGHT SECTOR on S.O.S. LINES. Situation normal during the day & usual harassing fire carried out at night.	MW
"	14		Intr. return relief carried out in Battery in HARLEY STREET. Usual harassing fire carried out. Lt. R.H. PEACOCK left for U.K. on special leave 30 days.	MW
	15		Situation normal. Usual harassing fire carried out.	MW
	16		HARLEY STREET BATTY. which is in 42nd Divisional Area changed with a Battery in SUSSEX TRENCH held by 42nd Division in our area. Usual harassing fire carried out at night. Lt. H.R. WHITTINGTON attached to Coy. as 2/3/c.	MW
	17		Situation normal. Usual harassing fire carried out.	MW
	18		Inspection of Transport by G.O.C. G.O.C. remarked a good turn out. Situation in the line normal. Usual harassing fire carried out.	MW

Army Form C. 2118.

WAR DIARY
INTELLIGENCE SUMMARY
(Erase heading not required.)

Place	Date	Hour	Summary of Events and Information	Remarks and references to Appendices
NOYELLES	19-20		Situation normal. Usual Harassing fire carried out.	ML-
"	21		Instruction relief carried out of RIGHT SECTOR. Usual Harassing fire.	ML-
"	22		G.S.O.I, D.M.G.O. & Capt. Low inspected VILLAGE LINE. Usual Harassing fire.	ML-
"	23		Situation normal. Usual Harassing fire carried out.	ML-
	24		2.Lt HEYWOOD reported for duty from 177 M.G.Coy. 500 rounds fired by RIGHT SECTOR GUNS in response to S.O.S. Usual Harassing fire carried out.	ML-
	25-27		Situation Normal. Harassing fire carried out each night.	ML-

Army Form C. 2118.

WAR DIARY
INTELLIGENCE SUMMARY
(Erase heading not required.)

Instructions regarding War Diaries and Intelligence Summaries are contained in F. S. Regs., Part II. and the Staff Manual respectively. Title Pages will be prepared in manuscript.

Place	Date	Hour	Summary of Events and Information	Remarks and references to Appendices
NOYELLES	28		Inter section relief of LEFT SECTOR. (BATTY in BUSSEX TRENCH) Harassing fire carried out according to programme.	MH
	29		Situation normal. Harassing fire carried out according to programme.	MH
	30		2 Officers 35 O.R. 11 horses & 3 limbers reporting reported to replace the section sent overseas. Officers Lt PARBURY and Lt DAVENPORT. Harassing fire carried out according to programme.	MH
	31		Situation normal. Harassing fire carried out according to programme.	MH
			During the whole month a considerable amount of work was done by the Company on the VILLAGE LINE. — Emplacements cleaned & repaired & several open emplacements were put in. All emplacements were brought up to their full complement of ammunition. Two A.A. Machine guns were constantly in action during the month.	

M/N[signature]
Comdg. 178 M.G. Coy.

Army Form C. 2118.

WAR DIARY
~~INTELLIGENCE SUMMARY.~~
(Erase heading not required.)

WAR DIARY

of

No 8 M.G. Coy.

from 1st – 31st January 1918.

Army Form C. 2118.

WAR DIARY

INTELLIGENCE SUMMARY.

(Erase heading not required.)

Instructions regarding War Diaries and Intelligence Summaries are contained in F. S. Regs., Part II. and the Staff Manual respectively. Title pages will be prepared in manuscript.

Place	Date	Hour	Summary of Events and Information	Remarks and references to Appendices
NOYELLES	1/1/18		Brought in the New Year with 10 minutes fire from "A" Batty on LEFT SECTOR. Night firing programme carried out.	WW.
	2/1/18		Enemy attempted to a raid with about 150 men "fronte CITÉ STELIE. Raid beaten off with casualties leaving prisoners in our hands. In response to S.O.S. in connection with the raid RIGHT SECTOR fired 1000 rounds. Night firing programme carried out. No.1 Team of the new Section went into the line for instruction.	WW.
	3/1/18		Situation normal. Night firing programme carried out.	WW.
	4/1/18		Instruction relief carried out on RIGHT SECTOR. Night firing programme carried out.	WW.
	5/1/18		Situation normal - nothing to report. Usual night firing programme carried out.	WW.

WAR DIARY
or
INTELLIGENCE SUMMARY.

Army Form C. 2118.

Place	Date	Hour	Summary of Events and Information	Remarks and references to Appendices
NOYELLES	6/1/17		N°s 2, 3, & 4 teams of new section went into the line for instruction. N°s 2 & 3 attached to our "A" Batty. N°4 attached to 138 M.G. Coy for 24 hours. 4 Artillery N.C.O's attached to A Batty for 24 hours for instruction. Usual night firing programme carried out.	
	7th		Situation normal. Usual night firing programme carried out.	
	9th		New section known as N°2 inspected by G.O.C. Night firing programme carried out.	
	10th		The positions V.H.5 and V.H.8 in the VILLAGE LINE reoccupied by 2 Teams of N°2 Section. Lt DAVENPORT in command. H.2. @ "A" Batty. Usual night firing programme carried out.	
	11th		Instruction relief carried out with "A" Batty. Usual night firing programme carried out. The additional emplacement V.25 occupied in VILLAGE LINE.	

WAR DIARY
INTELLIGENCE SUMMARY.

(Erase heading not required.)

Army Form C. 2118.

Instructions regarding War Diaries and Intelligence Summaries are contained in F. S. Regs., Part II. and the Staff Manual respectively. Title pages will be prepared in manuscript.

Place	Date	Hour	Summary of Events and Information	Remarks and references to Appendices
NOYELLES	12th		The following alterations carried out in position of guns in RIGHT SECTOR. Gun known as "POSEN" to "New Champagne" position, gun in MEATH TRENCH, opening of MEATH TRENCH, gun in temporary position in MEATH TRENCH moved to "Champagne" position in CHALK PIT ALLEY. Usual night firing programme carried out.	MW.
	13		Situation normal. Information received re relief of present division by 11 Division. Night firing programme carried out.	MW.
	14		Visited by O.C. 33 M.G. Coy. & 260 M.G. Coy. who will take over guns held by this Coy. Night firing programme carried out.	MW.
	15		Visited by O.C. 32 M.G. Coy. who is taking over guns held by this Coy. Relief as arranged cancelled owing to "thaw/precautions". Night firing programme carried out.	MW.

Army Form C. 2118.

WAR DIARY

INTELLIGENCE SUMMARY.

(Erase heading not required.)

Instructions regarding War Diaries and Intelligence Summaries are contained in F. S. Regs., Part II. and the Staff Manual respectively. Title pages will be prepared in manuscript.

Place	Date	Hour	Summary of Events and Information	Remarks and references to Appendices
NOYELLES	16th-20th		Situation normal. Night firing programme duly carried out. March & Relief table for No. 9 Companies received.	M.L.
	21st		"A" Batty & V.45 relieved by No. 250 M.G. Coy.	M.L.
	22-24		Situation normal. No night firing by this Company	M.L.
CHOQUES	25		V.45 & V.25 relieved by 32 M.G. Coy. R.40, 41, 42 relieved by 33 M.G. Coy. Company marched 6 Billets at CHOQUES.	M.L.
	26-31.		Company started training chiefly Squad drill & Rifle drill.	M.L.

W. Tipart & Soloft:
Comdg. 178 M.G. Coy.

WAR DIARY

of 178 M.G. Coy.

for 1st — 28th February.

WAR DIARY
INTELLIGENCE SUMMARY.
(Erase heading not required.)

Army Form C. 2118.

Place	Date	Hour	Summary of Events and Information	Remarks and references to Appendices
CHOQUES	1st -7th July		Company in training at CHOQUES — Squad & Arms drill, Elementary gun drill & Barrage drill. There was no suitable ground for Limber drill. 1 Officer reinforcement Lt FLETCHER reported.	
HURIONVILLE	8.		Divisional tactical route march, this Company was attached to the 139 Infantry Brigade and moved into their area. H.Q. and billets at HURIONVILLE.	
BEAUMETZ LES AIRES	9.		Company marched with 139 Bde. Group in accordance with Divisional Scheme to billet the Company at PTIGNY but on reaching there it was found there was no room & the Company was forced to this village. A Cooker was attached to the Company for the march & proved invaluable. Hot tea & hot dinners were served during the march. This would have been impossible without the cooker and as the Company did not reach billets till 10 P.M.	

(A/7092). W1. W12359/M1293. 750,000. 1/17. D. D. & L., Ld. Forms/C.2118/14.

WAR DIARY
or
INTELLIGENCE SUMMARY.

Army Form C. 2118.

Place	Date	Hour	Summary of Events and Information	Remarks and references to Appendices
			the state of the men if they had no hot meal can be imagined during the scheme the Company marched "Action expected" this proved to be more tiring on the men than when marching Action not expected.	
BEAUMETZ LES AIRES	10-27		These days were spent in training & forming the M.G. Battalion. 20 men were drawn from the other men and attached to this Company with a view to transfer to the M.G.C. all men fired a short musketry course during training & a fair amount of Lewis Gun & Rock drill accomplished	
do	28		The M.G. Battalion was officially formed. C.O. Col HEWITT 2/c Major KYBURN Adj Capt. DICKENS This Company will now be known as "D" Coy. 46th. Div. M.G. Batt.	W Hughes Lt Col R.C. 176 In E Bdy

WAR DIARY
or
INTELLIGENCE SUMMARY.

Army Form C. 2118.

WAR DIARY of 178 M.G. Coy for January 1st–28th

WAR DIARY

INTELLIGENCE SUMMARY

Place	Date	Hour	Summary of Events and Information	Remarks and references to Appendices
CHOQUES	1st /Feb		Company in training at CHOQUES - Squad & Arms Drill. Elementary Gun Drill & Barrage Drill. There was no suitable ground for Lumbar Drill. 1 Officer reinforcement Lt FLETCHER reported.	
HURIONVILLE	8		Proceeded tactical route march. This Company was attached to the 139 Infantry Brigade and moved into their area. H.Q. and billets at HURIONVILLE.	
BEAUMETZ LES AIRES	9		Company marched with 139 Bde group in accordance with Divisional scheme to BEAUMETZ LES AIRES. It was originally intended to billet the Company at PTIGNY but on reaching there found there was no room & the Company was bussed to this village. A cooker was attached to the Company for the march & proved invaluable. Hot tea & hot dinners were served during the march. This would have been impossible without the cooker and as the Company did not reach billets till 11.30 P.M.	

Place	Date	Hour	Summary of Events and Information	Remarks and references to Appendices
			the state of the men if they had had no hot meal can be imagined. During the scheme the Company marched "Action expected". This proved to be more tiring on the men than ordinary marching where Action not expected.	
BEAUMERE LES AIRES	10- 2?/		These days were spent in training & forming the M.G. Battalion. 30 men were drawn from the Division and attached to this Company with a view to transfer to the M.G.C. all such were ? short, mostly by reason of weak knees & ? war amount of ? ? broken toes & flat feet these was accomplished	
	28		The M.G. Battalion was an officially formed CO Col HEWITT 2/C Major KYBURN Adj Capt DICKENS This Company will now be known as "D" Coy 44th M.G. Bn.	

www.ingramcontent.com/pod-product-compliance
Lightning Source LLC
Chambersburg PA
CBHW081555160426
43191CB00011B/1939